AMERICAN PHILOSOPHY

THE BASICS

What is it that makes American philosophy unique? *American Philosophy: The Basics* answers this question by tracing the history of American thought from early Calvinists to the New England Transcendentalists and from contract theory to contemporary African American philosophy. This lively and compelling book introduces readers to:

- some of the most important thinkers in American history including Edwards, Paine, Peirce, Kuhn, West, and many more
- developments in five key areas of thought: epistemology, metaphysics, religion and ethics, social philosophy, and political philosophy
- contributions of American women, African Americans, and Native Americans.

Featuring suggestions for further reading and assuming no prior knowledge of philosophy, this is an ideal first introduction for anyone studying or interested in the history of American thought.

Nancy Stanlick is Associate Professor of Philosophy and Assistant Dean at the College of Arts and Humanities, University of Central Florida, USA.

D0140040

The Basics

AMERICAN PHILOSOPHY
THE BASICS

Nancy Stanlick

Routledge
Taylor & Francis Group

LONDON AND NEW YORK

First published 2013
by Routledge
2 Park Square, Milton Park, Abingdon, Oxon OX14 4RN

Simultaneously published in the USA and Canada
by Routledge
711 Third Avenue, New York, NY 10017

Routledge is an imprint of the Taylor & Francis Group, an informa business

British Library Cataloguing in Publication Data
A catalogue record for this book is available from the British Library

Library of Congress Cataloging in Publication Data
Stanlick, Nancy A.
American philosophy : the basics / Nancy Stanlick.
p. cm. – (The basics updated)
Includes bibliographical references.
1. Philosophy, American–History. I. Title.
B851.S73 2013
191–dc23
2012020528

ISBN: 978-0-415-68972-4 (hbk)
ISBN: 978-0-415-68970-0 (pbk)
ISBN: 978-0-203-08016-0 (ebk)

Typeset in Bembo
by Taylor & Francis Books

MIX
Paper from
responsible sources
FSC® C004839

Printed and bound in Great Britain by the MPG Books Group

For my professors who made it possible, and for my students who make it all worthwhile.

CONTENTS

PREFACE

I wish to thank my students at the University of Central Florida who
have over the years taken my course in American philosophy for their
questions, comments, and interest. I also wish to thank my friend and
mentor Bruce Silver for reading and commenting on several sections
and chapters of this book and for offering advice and encouragement
to me in many ways over many years. I am grateful to two of my
advanced undergraduate students who helped me to compile information for Chapters 7 and 8. Stephen Oldham and Dominique
Greene-Sanders took my American philosophy course and spent part
of the summer of 2011 doing background research on Native
American, African American, and American feminist philosophy.
Ann Maukonen, my former student and current colleague, compiled
much of the index and helped to prepare the glossary. I thank her
more than she will ever know. Karen Jaggar offered to assist with
index and glossary entries for Chapters 5 and 6, and to her I extend
my heartfelt thanks for stepping in to help. Thanks to the Departments
of Philosophy at the University of South Florida and the University
of Central Florida for the education I received and the opportunity
to educate others. And finally, thank you to my family who has put
up with this absent-minded professor and provided encouragement
that "it will be done soon" for the past two years.

Nancy Stanlick
Orlando, Florida, 2012
Email: Nancy.Stanlick@ucf.edu
Website: http://pegasus.cc.ucf.edu/~stanlick

INTRODUCTION

This book about American philosophy might be received by some as a bit short on philosophy. Some might claim that there is too little philosophy in it because many of the thinkers whose works I review are not really philosophers and their ideas are insufficiently philosophical. Perhaps their conception of philosophy, and especially their conception of American philosophy, is too narrow and restrictive.

A look at the history of Western philosophy takes us to times and places where who counts as a philosopher and what counts as philosophy evolves. Hesiod was an ancient Greek poet, but references to his *Theogony* regularly appear in books on Greek philosophy. It is possible that Plato would not recognize as philosophical some elements of Descartes' work and perhaps Benjamin Franklin looks non-philosophical to twentieth-century analytical philosophers. That someone might not be generally accepted as a philosopher by one group or tradition does not mean that the person's ideas have not influenced thought and action or that the person's ideas are not part of a system of thought leading to "Big Questions" that philosophers often ask.

Benjamin Franklin wrote on the **problem of evil** and the existence of God. Thomas Jefferson borrowed from Locke's **social contract theory** to write the Declaration of Independence. Emma Goldman's

anarchist Marxism led her to argue against **Puritanism** and patriotism. If Thomas Paine is discounted as a philosopher because his arguments are sometimes weak, then we must discount Descartes because some of his arguments are unconvincing and questionable. We accept Marx as a philosopher because of the form and content of his arguments about economic conditions and their effects on people and politics and we accept Robert Nozick as a philosopher for similar reasons. If philosophical ideas are the intellectual impetus for human understanding and action about reality, knowledge, and the good life, then the American thinkers and writers whose works and ideas are part of the content of this book are as much philosophers as Plato and Aristotle or René Descartes and John Locke.

From the **Great Awakening**'s Jonathan Edwards to the **Enlightenment**'s Thomas Paine, from the **Transcendentalist**'s Emerson to the **abolitionism** of Frederick Douglass, and from Emma Goldman's **anarchism** to the **philosophy of love** in Martin Luther King, Jr.'s civil rights activism, and from the Native American's connection to nature to the American feminist's **ethics of care**, the thinkers represented here have changed the landscape of American thought in many ways. If the influence of ideas on human understanding and human action is a mark of philosophy, then American philosophers and speculative thinkers are as much at home in philosophy as Plato or Descartes, and they deserve to be called philosophers.

What is American philosophy? To answer this question it is necessary to know something about philosophy and then to proceed to what is distinct, unique, and important about *American* philosophy. There are many different branches of philosophy and types of philosophical inquiry. American philosophy deals with all of them.

"Philosophy" may be variously described, but one may begin by thinking of it as the act of wondering. If that is vague, perhaps defining philosophy by describing some of the subjects about which philosophers write and speak will be sufficient. Philosophers study **epistemology**, **logic**, **metaphysics**, **ethics**, **philosophy of religion**, **social philosophy**, and **political philosophy**, among other subjects. Describing some of the branches of philosophical inquiry helps a bit in getting a grasp of what philosophers do and what philosophy is all about.

In the Western tradition, philosophy is a way of thinking about ideas that is usually characterized by reasoned inquiry into the nature and value of **argument**s and conclusions concerning issues in metaphysics, epistemology, and ethics, together with questions and analyses of arguments about the existence of God, the aims of science, and the legitimization of political systems. Philosophy may be defined as a system and process of creating and analyzing arguments and positions about these issues. Philosophers engage in analysis of ideas, concepts, principles, and problems to try to understand the nature of things. They do this through arguments. No matter what the position or idea, to be engaged in philosophical inquiry is to argue for claims, to provide reasons and justifications to believe that claims are true, not simply assert them as "true" or as mere facts.

All areas of human inquiry deal in some way with arguments, so it is important also to note that philosophy is certainly different from the sciences and from technical fields even though its subject matter may be in part shared with other disciplines. Physicists often deal with questions about the nature of reality, but the way in which they go about answering them is much different from what is usually done in philosophy. Where a physicist will use the scientific method and quantify data, philosophers often seek qualitative analysis of ideas and arguments to formulate answers to questions about the reason for being and the meaning of existence. Where the lawyer seeks to establish grounds for determining whether a defendant is guilty of a crime, the philosopher may instead be more concerned with the conditions of moral and legal responsibility, whether a person acts freely at all, and what it means and implies to talk about freedom and responsibility.

BRANCHES OF PHILOSOPHY

Epistemology is the theory of knowledge. **Philosophy of science** in this book is combined with epistemology because science and its methods are connected to questions of the type, applicability, reliability, and quality of knowledge claims. Among major questions or problems in epistemology are the distinction between knowledge and belief, the purposes of inquiry, whether there are **innate ideas** or whether all ideas arise through experience, whether **skepticism** is warranted and whether there are truths that can be known with absolute certainty, and which method of obtaining knowledge is most efficient and reliable. American philosophers tend to wonder what we can do with epistemological concepts and how knowledge of truth leads to productive results.

Metaphysics concerns issues such as the nature of reality or the fundamental question of what is real or existent. For an American **Pragmatist**, to determine what is meaningful and suitable as a subject of inquiry requires that we determine what difference thinking and theorizing about such things will make. On the whole, American philosophers tend toward finding the "cash value" or use of ideas. In other words, they wonder what concrete difference it would make if some position on the nature of reality is true.

Philosophy of religion is easily considered part of metaphysics or part of ethics. For our purposes, philosophy of religion sometimes appears in chapters combined with metaphysics and at other times combined with ethics, depending on the chapter's focus and content. Questions from philosophy of religion are common in American thought and have implications beyond questions concerning God and religion and move into ethical, social, and political life. It is therefore useful and productive for understanding many aspects of American philosophy to consider the impact and effects of beliefs and claims about God, religion, and theology on the development of American thought. Issues arising in philosophy of religion range from arguments for the existence of God to attempts to solve the problem of evil, and from questions about the nature of religious belief to the role of ritual in religious practice. In American philosophy, concerns about religion often turn toward the effects of belief on individual people or on a community. American philosophers tend to use religion for various practical purposes to further other philosophical ends or goals, or they provide justifications or criticisms of it with specific attention to the ways in which religious belief or its absence affects people's lives and happiness.

Ethics, a branch of philosophy concerned with the good, the right, happiness, duty, and human character, has affinities to all the other branches of philosophy. Some of the moral views in American thought to which attention is directed in this book are the concepts of human nature, moral arguments against slavery and oppression, conceptions of the nature of human happiness and the goal of human life, and the distinctions and differences between types of ethical theories and the ways in which they affect action.

Social and political philosophy are distinct, but in this book they appear together as subsections of relevant chapters. This is the case because American social and political thought are not easily separable. From the American revolutionaries all the way to contemporary Pragmatists, Native American and African American philosophers, issues of rights, justice, and equality take center stage. It is not always the case that the issues take center stage in the same way, or with the same reasoning, or even with the same consequences, but there is always a place for social thought in American philosophy. Discussion and argument concerning the value, justification, power, and legitimacy of government occupy American philosophers and theorists. Whatever the issues in American political thought, American philosophers tend to focus on the practical, the useful, and a consideration of how answers to political questions will affect the ways in which human beings live their lives.

AMERICAN PHILOSOPHY

Rich white men, poor Southern former slaves, Christian women, a displaced British pamphleteer, a **Calvinist** preacher, university professors, Marxists and anarchists, **egoists** and communitarians, all grace the history of American thought. Their ideas make the American experience come alive. American philosophy and philosophers are distinct in the pursuit of the application of philosophy to lives played out on the American stage.

Most American philosophers concentrate on the concrete difference that will be made by our conceptions, arguments, and ideas in the lives of individual human beings and groups. This is not to say that American philosophers disparage or fail to appreciate understanding a concept or inquiring into a topic for intellectual satisfaction, but the tendency of American philosophers is still the practical, the useful, and the concrete. American philosophers tend to ask what we can *do* with theories, principles, and arguments.

CONCLUSION AND PLAN OF THE BOOK

This book is intended as an overview of the history of American philosophy with emphasis on the themes of the practicality of philosophical ideas, revolution and evolution (change and reform in American thought), and a critical and constructive eye on issues involving justice, rights, and equality. It is inevitable that in a book intended as an introduction to a broad topic there will be some issue or philosopher, some argument or thinker, who will be omitted. It may also be that an idea or thinker is included that some may think should have been left out. I have included some of the major figures and ideas in the development of American philosophy that are particularly relevant to the themes of this book. Given page restrictions and thematic boundaries, it is not possible to include everything or everyone. I have tried, however, to present a consistent view of the history of American philosophy. Part of the goal of this book is to explain what makes American philosophy a national or cultural philosophical tradition.

Discussing the ideas and theories in each chapter by organizing and characterizing them by categories will easily allow the reader to cross-reference ideas between and among chapters. For example, Jonathan Edwards' epistemology can be easily compared with the epistemology of the Pragmatists, and the revolutionary founders' conceptions of freedom and justice in Chapter 3 can be compared with contemporary communitarian social and political thought in Chapter 8. Occasionally, chronological ordering of philosophers and their works overlap between chapters because the lives of philosophers with distinct and different interests also overlap. To maintain continuity, for example, Richard Rorty is part of Chapter 6 on the early American Pragmatists even though he was a late twentieth-century philosopher whose work is concurrent with that of many philosophers discussed in Chapters 7 and 8. A glossary appears at the end of the book for additional clarification of terms and concepts, which are shown in bold in their first or primary occurrences in the main text.

Each chapter is centered on a development in American thought that has had a significant impact on the history of Western philosophy or on the American experience, or both. Each chapter is focused on some figures concerning a particular aspect or topic in American philosophy with attention to major developments within that topic. The following is a general plan or overview of the subsequent chapters.

Chapter 2 involves themes and problems in the philosophy of Jonathan Edwards, a representative of the Calvinist tradition and the

First American Great Awakening. Included is an attempt to situate Edwards' thought in the larger history of Western philosophy from which many of his ideas are derived and from which some diverge. Chapter 3 centers on revolutionary American thinking of the Enlightenment including that of Thomas Paine, Benjamin Franklin, John Adams, and the **Federalists**.

Chapter 4 takes us beyond the original American revolution with ideas influenced by the experiences of those who were discounted or ignored in the promises of the American Revolution. American women, slaves, and abolitionists are at the center of this chapter, including William Lloyd Garrison, Frederick Douglass, Angelina and Sarah Grimké, and Elizabeth Cady Stanton, all of whom were concerned to extend the notion of what it is to be fully human and to be entitled to respect, liberties, and full participation in the American experience outlined by the founders of the new American republic. They extend the theoretical underpinnings of the American Revolution to help build a better life and future for all Americans, not just those of privilege and traditional power.

Chapter 5 continues the theme of Chapter 4, but goes beyond it in the work of Ralph Waldo Emerson and Henry David Thoreau, the two best known and prolific writers among the Transcendentalists. Emerson and Thoreau are well-known for ruggedly individualistic ideas, revolutionary thinking in moral and political realms, and insistence upon a unique look at the American experience and the obligation of Americans to re-invent themselves in a particularly and uniquely American way. The work of the Transcendentalists theorizing about independence, freedom, and fairness is directed against the blandly ordinary and largely pathetic tendencies of people to follow the crowd rather than to forge their own tools of growth to create a uniquely American experience. Closing Chapter 5 is the continuing work of reform of W. E. B. Du Bois and Emma Goldman on African American philosophy and radical Marxist anarchism.

Chapter 6 concerns American Pragmatism and four of its primary proponents (Charles Sanders Peirce, William James, John Dewey, and Richard Rorty). Pragmatists insist on the "practical" in all matters, whether they are epistemological, metaphysical, religious, moral, social, or political. For the pragmatists, the point is to change the world, not to try in some vaguely analytical fashion to "understand" it without making understanding count in the realm of action. Like the revolutionary Americans of the eighteenth century, the American Pragmatists argued to produce real, significant, revolutionary, and substantial change in ways of understanding, being, and doing.

Chapter 7, part one of recent developments in American philosophy, deals with some major developments in American epistemology and philosophy of science and an introduction to the unity of Native American philosophy. Chapter 8, the second part of recent developments in American philosophy, closes this book with contemporary social and political thought, **feminist ethics**, and African American philosophy.

Ethics, social philosophy, and political philosophy tend to be heavily represented in American philosophy and in the works of the thinkers whose ideas populate the pages of this book. It is perhaps the case that for American philosophy, understanding what there is, what we know, and our relationship, if any, to a god or gods inform our lives of action in seeking to live in a progressive, peaceful, just, and productive society.

FURTHER READING

For an overview of Western philosophy, Nigel Warburton's *Philosophy: The Basics*, 4th ed. (London: Routledge, 2004) is very useful. Nicholas Bunnin and E. P. Tsui-James (eds.), *The Blackwell Companion to Philosophy*, 2nd ed. (Malden, MA: Blackwell, 2003) is a collection of essays on major branches of philosophy. Arthur Danto's *Connections to the World* (New York: Harper & Row, 1989) is an engaging overview of the history of Western thought.

Useful anthologies in American philosophy include L. Harris, S. Pratt, and A. Waters' *American Philosophies* (Oxford: Blackwell, 2002) which also includes selections from Native American philosophers; Nancy Stanlick and Bruce Silver's *Philosophy in America: Selected Readings, Volume I* (Upper Saddle River, NJ: Pearson Prentice Hall, 2004) is a collection of works in American philosophy centered on optimism, individualism, and reform. John Stuhr's *Classical American Philosophy* (New York: Oxford University Press,

1987) and *Pragmatism and Classical American Philosophy* (New York: Oxford, 2000) are important for centering on American Pragmatism.

Internet resources on American philosophy are found on many sites devoted to specific American philosophers or movements in American thought, but a good place to start is always the *Stanford Encyclopedia of Philosophy* (http://plato.stanford.edu).

THE GENESIS OF EURO-AMERICAN PHILOSOPHY

Jonathan Edwards (1703–58) is the first systematic European-American philosopher. Edwards' work in epistemology and science, in philosophy of religion, and in metaphysics is the primary concern of this chapter. The ideas of Jonathan Edwards derive from and contribute to the Great Awakening in America. Influenced by the independent spirit of the British colonists, the Great Awakening moved people toward a religious and emotional "sense" in place of formalized religious knowledge, and toward acceptance of an individual relationship with God rather than a distant and doctrine-bound apprehension of religious truth and practice.

EPISTEMOLOGY, SCIENTIFIC KNOWLEDGE, AND RELIGIOUS TRUTH

Even though Edwards was a **religious enthusiast**, he was influenced by the epistemology of John Locke and the metaphysics of George Berkeley, who were British **empiricists**. He contended that all ideas arise through experience, but that we cannot transcend ideas derived from experience to the knowledge of things as they are. Beyond the limits of Locke's philosophy, Edwards claimed that **the "elect"** have a "sixth sense," a **sense of the heart**, that allows them to apprehend the true nature of God.

It is important to distinguish between the *origin* of ideas and the *character* of knowledge both for Locke and for Edwards. For Locke, in the *Essay Concerning Human Understanding* (1690), ideas arise through sense experience. Knowledge, however, goes beyond experience and is the notice the mind takes of the agreement or disagreement between ideas. So knowledge is about relationships between and among ideas. It is not about "things." Edwards agreed. Interestingly, however, Locke argued that we could know with probability that material objects exist while at the same time arguing that we really have no strict knowledge of external objects at all. Edwards recognized the problem with this view and adopted instead a view similar to George Berkeley's **idealism**.

George Berkeley argued that material objects do not exist and that, ultimately, all of reality exists in the mind of God. Combining elements of Locke and Berkeley, Edwards held that truth is consistency of our ideas with the ideas of God. Another way to put it is that truth is agreement of ideas with things as they are. What we call material things exist only mentally (i.e., ultimately in the mind of God) and that, as a corollary, "God is Truth itself." What is in the mind of God is what is real and science studies what is real. If this is true, Edwards concludes, as Berkeley did, that science and theology cannot be in conflict with each other.

An early indication that Edwards thought studying nature and engaging in scientific observation are consistent with religious truth – and indeed, for Edwards, will produce knowledge about God – is in his short essay, "The Spider Letter" (1723). Edwards carefully observed and made meticulous notes on the life cycles and activities of spiders, concluding that God's goodness is evident in all of it, from the ability of the spiders to spin webs to providing for the spiders so that they might experience pleasure. All of this means that in observing nature we can find the goodness and glory of God.

The work of God found in nature is part of the **teleological argument** for God's existence. Edwards found no need to argue that God exists, but his observations of nature and the conclusions he reached are fully consistent with that argument. The teleological argument is consistent with the work of the very pious Edwards and, as we will see in Chapter 3, also with the less than pious Thomas Paine. This argument for God's existence is consistent with the beliefs of those who contend that God is an active force in individual lives as well as for those who, like the **Deists** of the late eighteenth century, think of God as a detached grand watchmaker. All who adopt the teleological argument accept several of its basic tenets such as a rejection of chance or random occurrences in the natural world and acceptance of the **principle of universal causation**.

The argument has a simple and straightforward structure. We observe that there are things or beings in the world that are fit for a particular purpose. Some of these things or beings lack intelligence. Things that lack intelligence cannot move themselves toward goals or purposes. There must be something else that moves them since it is not reasonable to assume that regularity would come about as the result of chance or random occurrence. Therefore, there must be an intelligent designer that gives to unintelligent things their goals and purposes. The intelligent designer is identified as God.

This argument fits well with Edwards' contention in the "Spider Letter" that there is order and an obvious plan even in the mere activities and lives of spiders. The plan is evidence of the goodness and glory of God.

Even if observation of nature can lead to the conclusion – or if it can solidify the conclusion already reached – that God exists, it is not sufficient to acquire the ultimate knowledge which God's special creation, human beings, are capable of obtaining. To reach the heights of knowledge taking human beings beyond mere ideas and inferences based on them to intuitive and enlightened religious knowledge that only the "elect" can attain requires a "sense of the heart," the meaning and implications of which Edwards discusses in "A Divine and Supernatural Light" (1734) and *A Treatise Concerning Religious Affections* (1746).

To attain complete and transformative knowledge of God is to possess and employ the "holy affections" and the "sense of the heart." The sense of the heart allows one to acquire and understand ideas beyond the capacity of the five senses and beyond the comprehension of ordinary humans. Having the sense of the heart indicates that the receiver is one of the elect who will look upon the face of God, experience salvation, and apprehend ultimate beauty and reality in the Universe.

The sense of the heart is not passive like ordinary organs of sense. Ordinary experience may give one the *conviction* that God exists, but the sense of the heart provides *complete knowledge* through perception of the beauty and holiness of God. It is one thing to be told or to have the opinion that God *is*; it is a completely different experience to apprehend completely the meaning of this truth. The transformed human becomes a saint, one of the elect who does not sit idly in contemplation of God, but actively wills union with God. The gift of grace provides the converted saint access to supernatural affections (feelings, which are themselves experiences) and are proof that the recipient is one of the elect, a person saved from the tainted, worldly existence to which the unconverted are inseparably connected in this life.

METAPHYSICS: REALITY, THE WILL, AND RELIGION

Unfortunately for the sinner, extraordinary knowledge is available only to the converted saint. It remains part of the beauty and justice of the universe that unconverted sinners know as much as they can about the consequences of sinfulness and understand the gravity of their ultimate plight. To educate the irremediably unconverted and to convert those for whom there is hope, Edwards' most well-known sermon, "Sinners in the Hands of an Angry God" (1741), centers on the absolute sovereignty of God and what this means for our understanding of reality and our place in Creation.

There are four primary conclusions to be reached from "Sinners in the Hands of an Angry God." First, every human being is a sinner and has no reason to expect mercy from God. Second, there is absolutely nothing anyone can do to earn or merit salvation. Third, all of Creation is absolutely and utterly dependent upon God *and*, fourth, dependency of all things is evidence of God's ultimate sovereignty.

The first conclusion is a clear and undeniable statement of Calvinist theology. The other three conclusions, however, are important for understanding the manner in which the sovereignty of God is established and known, and why it is necessary that we are not possessed of free will but that we are, in the final analysis, still responsible for what we do.

Design in the universe is an indication of the dependency of all things on God. If God provides the reason for a thing's being and all that is needed for created beings to live and thrive, everything is completely dependent upon God. Therefore, there is nothing **autonomous** in the universe. Only God is an autonomous being and rules the universe according to laws of his own creation. Created beings are *subject to* the laws and decrees of God but have nothing to do with changing things as they were meant by God to be.

The explicit message of "Sinners in the Hands of an Angry God" is not uplifting. Edwards described human beings as utterly and completely sinful, ulcerous, sordid, loathesome, abhorrent, abominable, and corrupt. We are a burden on Creation. We should expect – and we deserve – absolutely nothing from God. The only reason that we are not at this moment cast into the fiery pit of Hell is that God keeps us from falling into it. It is only the few who convert and overcome the ugliness of their mere human existence who will delight in taking a place in Heaven. Those fortunate enough to be saved by unearned and undeserved grace are, therefore, ultimately and completely dependent upon God. No good works lead to salvation, so we have no power to effect salvation. In fact, for Edwards it is the reverse. The elect will behave and live in a way consistent with their exalted status. Salvation, just like damnation, is determined by God's sovereign and arbitrary will, indicating that God owes us nothing but that we owe God everything.

Two very important implications of Edwards' position on human dependency are that we are equal from the perspective of God and that we are not possessed of free will but we are, nonetheless, responsible for what we do. That human beings are equal from the perspective of God is unremarkable. What it means to be possessed of equality, however, is a completely different matter: we are all equal to each other in sinfulness and depravity.

If all humans are equal from the perspective of God, what do we make of converted saints? The answer is simple and straightforward. After conversion, the elect are no longer merely human. They are, instead, *super*natural human beings in sainthood. Equality with ordinary, unconverted men and women no longer applies to them.

Things being as they are and as they are meant to be leads to the especially contentious Edwardsian sense of freedom. Edwards' sermon on despicable sinners says we are radically dependent beings. *Enquiry into Freedom of the Will* (1754) tells us we are powerless to change the course of events. We are, however, free and responsible for all the choices we make.

Edwards' concern in *Enquiry into Freedom of the Will* is to reply to the Arminian view that we are radically free rather than radically dependent beings. The theory of **Arminian radical freedom** (developed by followers of the Dutch Calvinist theologian Jacobus Arminius) denies determination of the will and **predestination**. Both determination of the will and predestination are essential parts of Edwards' view of the sovereignty of God. So in Edwards' view, if humans had free will and the ability to alter the course of events in the world, it would indicate that God is not ultimately sovereign (i.e., that God is not ultimately powerful and not all knowing, both of which are inconsistent with the nature of God).

If everything that occurs must be exactly as it is and not otherwise and there was never any chance that what occurs could have been other than what it is, the question remains what the will is and how we can be responsible for what we do. Edwards' answer to the question regarding the nature of the will is complicated, but his answer to the question regarding moral responsibility for the choices we make is surprisingly aligned with common sense.

For Edwards, willing is nothing more than the act of choosing. Will, therefore, is not some mysterious organ in a body, a brain, or a mind. The will, which is a power, chooses based on the strongest motive. What appears to the actor to be good or best among supposed options is that on which the person acts, and that which is considered good or best is the motive of action. So the will is determined. But this does not mean that the *actor* cannot be free.

Regardless of the reason the actor prefers one thing over another, the essence of freedom for Edwards is the ability to do what one *chooses* to do. In other words, it makes no sense to talk of freedom of the will since the will must, like all other things, be determined by divine foreknowledge while a *person* is free when he is able to do what he desires to do. Alternately, the person is free when he is not hindered in doing what he wills to do. This is called **compatibilism**, such that freedom and **determinism** are consistent (i.e., compatible) with each other.

The compatibilist's explanation of the case is simple. Even though every event must have a cause, and the causal chain of events goes back indefinitely, the question of the freedom of the person is answered by understanding that a person is free when he is not kept from doing that which he wills to do. So, for example, if a person is in a locked room but does not know it is locked and that he cannot leave, but in addition the person does not *want* or *will* to leave, there is no reason to claim that he is *not free to leave* when he *does not want to leave*. It is when he wishes or wills to leave and cannot do so that he is constrained. But just so long as a person is able to do what he wishes or wills to do, he is free. Human beings are free when they act on motives and habits simply because they are *theirs*.

The looming question is whether this account of the nature of freedom and God's predetermination and predestination is consistent with moral responsibility. For Edwards, predetermination and predestination do not remove personal and individual responsibility for actions. The reason that people are responsible for what they choose to do is a common-sense and straightforward one. In ordinary cases we hold people responsible for what they do when they have done what they willed to do regardless of more distant or remote causes leading them to prefer one course of action over another. If a person is not impeded in acting as he wishes to act, we hold him responsible for what he does and offer praise or blame depending on whether the results of the choice are beneficial or not. If a person is impeded in acting as he wishes to act, we do not hold the person responsible for the results. It is as simple as that.

CRITICISMS

Edwards' Calvinist theology and philosophy constitute a **theodicy** in which whatever happens must happen the way it does, and given God's goodness and grace, everything happens for the best. But there remains in this **hard deterministic** and bleak view of humanity that there is something terribly wrong with a philosophy offering an explanation of the reality of the entire universe and a conception of knowledge and human action that render us nothing more than puppets of an ultimate being acting by its arbitrary will. It may make us wonder what is the point in living at all.

There is an answer to the question of the reason for our existence. We are part of the fullness, completeness, and glory of God – even when we are sordid, ulcerous, and despicable sinners. Being able to tell a story about our existence and about praise- and blameworthiness, and about whether we are saved or damned, may provide some intellectual satisfaction for those who are convinced that Edwards' position is true.

But conviction that one is right because one feels very strongly that he is in possession of the truth about the nature of God and religious knowledge is certainly not convincing to anyone but the believer. John Locke and David Hume both offered scathing criticisms of the status of religious enthusiasm of this and other sorts. Locke put the case succinctly in contending that even though revelation is from God and is therefore beyond doubt, we must still be careful about what we take to be true as revelation that it really is divine revelation. How can we be sure that the claims of the supposedly converted are not merely the result of wishful thinking supported by a strong feeling? Religious enthusiasts may think a "truth" is a revelation because they are persuaded that it is, and they believe it is a revelation because they believe it very strongly. In other words, the religious enthusiast argues in a circle.

Edwards' reasoning from the existence of nature to the existence and character of God is exceptionally weak. There is nothing in the character or existence of an effect indicating the nature of its cause, and many later thinkers in the history of American philosophy, including the Pragmatists, take issue with the use of the teleological argument when the **theory of evolution** explains many things more effectively. There are many people even in the twenty-first century who deny the theory of evolution. But the fact that they are convinced because they are convinced and find it repugnant to their beliefs to think otherwise is no good or rational reason to accept the theory of **intelligent design** as true. The facts do not support intelligent design, the theory is not testable, and since it carries its own evidence within itself, it is essentially insulated from criticism. It has the same status as belief in revelation.

There is nothing in Edwards' concept of human nature, and indeed in the nature of God, to offer any one of us except the saint any hope for the future. If human beings are sordid, sinful, ulcerous, and despicable, perhaps they deserve nothing more than what they get and what they have. On the other hand, there are very few ordinary American citizens and even fewer revolutionary American philosophers and speculative thinkers who will stand still and rest satisfied in being oppressed, hopeless, downtrodden, poor, and unworthy of anything better.

It may also be the case that Edwards' own contentions regarding the unmerited grace of God for the converted, and the merited damnation awaiting the unconverted, are inconsistent overall. If the converted do not deserve salvation because they are elected by God and have done nothing to warrant salvation, then why is it that sinners deserve punishment when their fate has been sealed by God just as much as the fate of the elect? It is evident that Edwards has an answer given his position on the nature of the relationship between free action and moral responsibility. Those who do as they ought to do and are among the converted receive reward from God just as those who do not do what they ought to do and are unconverted receive punishment from God just as they should. Further, those who do what they ought to do in this world are praised by other human beings for what they do when what they do is consistent with their character and it is done without constraint. And those who do not do what they ought to do, or who do what they ought not to do, are subject to blame by other human beings for what is consistent with their character and done without constraint.

The explanation of responsibility provided by the Calvinist makes perfectly good intellectual sense, but unfortunately, it does not convince anyone who inquires further and wonders whether it matters that we do what we wish or will to do when the motive of our actions is not determined by us. Human autonomy is completely absent from Edwards' reasons and conclusions leading to the thesis of the ultimate and radical dependency of human beings, and indeed of the entire universe, on the will of God.

CONCLUSION

The history of American philosophy would not be much of a history if the majority of American philosophers, activists, and speculative thinkers had retained or adopted Edwards' Calvinist stance. If they had, they certainly would not have been activists. Fortunately for all of us, a spirit of optimism and reform in this life overcomes the tidy world of Edwardsian dependency.

Most of the American philosophers and speculative thinkers after Edwards rejected the dismal view of Edwardsian Calvinism and all that it implies. But even if attitudes change and approaches to the world move from mere acceptance of the status quo to revolutionary action, there is still a sense in which Edwards' views on human equality are characteristic of the American penchant for change. Just as repentant sinners are changed and transformed by the mercy and grace of God, later thinkers, especially some of the revolutionaries whose ideas are considered in Chapters 3 and 4, and the New England Transcendentalists discussed in Chapter 5, take the concept of equality to new heights and see in it possibilities for radical and progressive change in American moral, social, and political contexts. The American Pragmatists (Chapter 6) continue the analysis of **absolutist** and **dualistic** tendencies in the history of Western thought using evolutionary theory and a progressive concept of democracy to argue for conclusions much different from those of Edwards.

Edwards' works express an absolutist and abstract philosophy rejected by the philosophers and speculative thinkers later in the history of American philosophy who embrace revolutionary thought, the practical application of philosophical ideas, and concern with socially important matters such as freedom, rights, and justice. It is those thinkers to whom the rest of this book is primarily devoted for their contributions to the revolutionary, evolutionary, practical application of philosophical concepts and reasoning.

FURTHER READING

For Edwards' philosophy generally, see Sang Hyun Lee, *The Philosophical Theology of Jonathan Edwards* (Princeton, NJ: Princeton University Press, 2000); for his theology, Michael J. McClymond and Gerald R. McDermott, *The Theology of Jonathan Edwards* (New York: Oxford University Press, 2012) and Michael J. McClymond, *Encounters with God: An Approach to the Theology of Jonathan Edwards* (New York: Oxford University Press, 1998). For the historical and cultural contexts of Edwards' work, an excellent source is Thomas S. Kidd, *The Great Awakening: The Roots of Evangelical Christianity in Colonial America* (New Haven: Yale University Press, 2007).

3

THE ENLIGHTENMENT REVOLUTIONARIES

REVOLUTIONARY THINKING

It did not take long for the pessimistic Calvinistic views of Edwards to give way to the revolutionary Enlightenment thought of Thomas Paine (1737–1809), Thomas Jefferson (1743–1826), Benjamin Franklin (1706–90), John Adams (1735–1826), and James Madison (1751–1836). The spirit of the Enlightenment took hold, displacing the **authoritarianism** of the Calvinist Great Awakening. While Edwards had respect for the new science of the Modern era and incorporated it into his philosophical system, the work of science and reason was for him relegated ultimately to justifications of religious faith and orthodoxy. Where Edwards celebrated the ability through human reason to understand problems associated with free will and determinism, reason took a back seat to religious enthusiasm in understanding our place in the world. Where Edwards saw sin and ulcerous humanity, the Enlightenment revolutionaries saw hope and dignity.

The rise of Modern science and the spirit of Enlightenment led American revolutionary thinkers to understand that autonomous human beings are not rightly held down by the weight of external power with dubious (or any) claims to authority and truth. Neither are they to be oppressed by stifling requirements and expectations of a political system keeping them in a condition of perpetual childhood, subject to a powerful government that claimed it knew better than they what was good for them and what they ought to do. The American Enlightenment revolutionaries were not content being subject to a government as far away from them in distance as in philosophical temperament, subject to traditions that did not fit their lives, and subject to religious beliefs, moral systems, and government forms that were inconsistent with their ideals.

Enlightenment thinking in Europe and America affected all realms of human inquiry and interest from science to religion and from ethics to politics. The effects of Enlightenment rationality should not be understated. Without Enlightenment, there would have been no America.

WHAT IS ENLIGHTENMENT?

Immanuel Kant, an eighteenth-century German philosopher and one of the chief expositors of Enlightenment rationality, explained what is alternately called "The **Age of Reason**" in his brief essay, "What is Enlightenment?" (1784). For Kant, Enlightenment is the emancipation of humanity from ignorance, error, and intellectual immaturity. It is characterized by confidence in human reason, trust in human autonomy, and belief in human dignity.

The rise of Modern science granted people the ability to solve problems through rational means and it allowed them to see that the world was much different from what they thought. Revolutionary events in science had occurred with Copernicus' rejection of the **geocentric theory** turning Aristotelian science upside down. The traditional view was that the Earth was the center of the universe and mankind was the ultimate creation on it. Being the "chosen" creation on the planet at the center of the universe, human beings were taught by the authority of the Church that everything was created for them, by God, and that the meaning of it all centered on humans, God, and salvation. The **heliocentric theory** challenged all that.

Scientific discoveries of various kinds sent a significant shock through Western society. Faith in the truth and authority of the past was weakened by exploration of lands and contact with people previously unknown to Europeans. Europeans were beginning to realize that their ways were not the only ways and that there were people around the world who did not look, act, or think like Europeans. More exposure to difference and diversity in thoughts, people, religions, practices, governments, and societies began to challenge the way things were and led people to revolt against the status quo in science, religion, ethics, politics, and other realms.

Add to all this the horrible treatment suffered by so many at the hands of absolute monarchs and unbalanced **Inquisitors** seeking to ensure that everyone conforms to their political or religious dogma or die, and human beings were at a breaking point. It was time in the seventeenth century to do something to effect positive and productive change in society and government. Science was breaking free from the chains of the authority of the Church, and rational human beings should be free from the authoritative chains of the state.

With Enlightenment, reason began to replace and augment religious faith and absolute and oppressive governments. It began to transform culture and society to promote human freedom and autonomy. That religion often promoted and encouraged ignorance and that governments often sank into absolutism did not lead Enlightenment thinkers to argue completely against either religion or government. But revolutionary thinking and action must be employed in all the realms in which oppression, ignorance, power, and authority threaten the dignity, value, and intelligence of human beings. This does not mean that the Age of Reason brings with it anarchy and an "anything goes" attitude. Enlightenment demands instead that old structures that are offensive to reason should be replaced by those that are consistent with reason. For the American Enlightenment, it is primarily its manifestations and effects in religion, ethics, social thought, and politics that are most prominent and important. Revolutionary thought in these realms grew from the early Modern era to the eighteenth-century Enlightenment thinkers who transformed a rag-tag association of farmers and statesmen, hunters and craftsmen, intellectuals and business owners into the largest and most successful experiment in democracy the world has ever known.

REVOLUTIONARY EPISTEMOLOGY, METAPHYSICS, AND METHOD

In place of the authoritarianism of Aristotelian science and the stilted education provided by the Church to those lucky enough to have any education at all, science was leading Western Europeans to declare independence from authority, tradition, and oppressive rule. The "**resolutive–compositive method**" was used by Descartes to find a firm foundation for the sciences. Hobbes used it to justify the contractarian conception of the legitimacy and power of government. Locke used it to argue for a government less powerful than that of Hobbes, and the American revolutionaries used it to argue for the right to engage in political revolution.

The resolutive-compositive method is simple and straightforward. A problem (a complex thing) is broken down into its smallest possible components so that the internal workings of a whole can be understood by analysis of its parts. For example, instead of assuming that the human body works in this or that way based on a cursory examination only of its external form, an anatomist sees benefit in dissecting the body to inspect all of its organs and parts.

It may be even more helpful to understand the resolutive-compositive method by explaining its use in the works of Descartes and Paine. Descartes was skeptical that what counted as knowledge deserved that name. What counted as knowledge in his time was largely the result of verification using **Aristotelian logic** to rehearse arguments and to take on faith or the authority of the Church or the state that this or that proposition, theory, or principle was true. Descartes, however, would not sit still for that. Instead, he proceeded through a mind experiment to dissect and analyze the concept of knowledge itself. He wanted to find the ultimate constituents of knowledge because understanding the parts of a thing would give rise to a better understanding of the whole.

Descartes found that engaging in **hyperbolic doubt** tears away dubious claims to knowledge to lead him to a new, clean, uncluttered starting point for the growth of knowledge. The new starting point was recognizing that "I am; I exist" is true. The Cartesian starting point is a rallying cry for all individualists and **rationalists** to come. Affirming the ultimate criterion of truth, the **criterion of clarity and distinctness**, led Descartes to something truly revolutionary: the conclusion that the individual knower is the guarantor of knowledge. It is not the Church, not the state, not tradition, not authority that guarantees knowledge. It is individual human beings using their own rational capacity. This is no small achievement. Up to the time of Descartes and Hobbes in the seventeenth century, the individual human being was not the creator or guarantor of knowledge or power. The individual was instead subject to knowledge and power and put into a position of less importance than the institutions and societies in which he existed. It is useful to keep in mind that the Aristotelian view from *Politics* and *Metaphysics* was essentially that for politics, the state is prior to the individual and that from a metaphysical point of view, the whole is prior to its parts.

Being "prior" does not mean that states literally exist before human beings or that complex wholes exist independently of their parts. It is that the state takes precedence over the individual, including individual goals, aspirations, desires, and dreams. The individual is swallowed up in the mechanism of the state to be a cog in a machine rather than an autonomous human being. The state is not given legitimacy by the people who are its subjects. The state gains legitimacy, instead, from its supposedly natural place superior to individuals. Similar considerations apply regarding knowledge. Individual pieces of knowledge have legitimacy by the edifice of knowledge itself, not the other way around. So an individual piece of information that does not fit well or at all into the reigning world view is rejected out of hand as blasphemous and obviously false. The system of thought already in place rejects any alternative view in principle, regardless of how or why the individual claim was derived or verified. For example, Galileo's discovery of the moons around Jupiter was to many people considered the height of irreligious speculation. It was called blasphemous, evil, and false. On the other hand, the application of the resolutive-compositive method makes it possible and acceptable to offer new ideas and ways of conceiving of truth. New ideas in the Modern world are to be tested, not rejected out of hand.

Paine and other political theorists of his time employed the new method of science in the social and political realms to create a new way of conceiving the relationship of the individual to the state. He analyzed the origins, legitimacy, function, purpose, and power of government by thinking about what we would conclude if we were to subject the concept of government to scientific method. Using a hypothetical "**state of nature**," we find that the elementary parts of governments are not kings, queens, dukes, and generals. All individual human beings who compose the state are its foundation. If this is true, then governments, formed from and by the people, are legitimate only when they are authorized by the people and take into account their desires, interests, and concerns. It is the interests of individual citizens, not only the "whole" or leaders, that are central to constructing and legitimizing governments. This is the intellectual justification for representative government, the right of the people to choose and establish the government under which they live.

The transformation of ways of thinking in the social realm challenges authority and tradition. The challenges include questioning the notion that people are subject *to* a government and turn to the notion that they are subjects *of* a government that they form by agreement with each other. Government is now the result of people coming to recognize and respect the inherent power, dignity, and rationality of human beings. Applying the new method of science causes transformations in ways of thinking and acting in science, morals, religion, and politics. It has monumental effects for the Enlightenment revolutionaries of America.

REVOLUTIONARY PHILOSOPHY OF RELIGION

Enlightenment reason applied to religious claims is no less revolutionary than the application of reason and method in science. Paine, Jefferson, and Franklin all found **Deism** a plausible and acceptable doctrine. For the Deist, God neither commands prayer nor expects ritualistic religious action. It is a religion without a Church and an attitude about Creation and our place in the world instead of a doctrine and set of rituals. Considering some of the ways in which American revolutionary Enlightenment thinking is applied to religious doctrines helps to shed light on further developments in other realms.

Among early American thinkers, Paine is probably the most vociferously critical regarding religion on the whole. In *The Age of Reason, Part I* (1794), Paine evaluated the consistency, effects, and legitimacy of religious doctrines on the conduct of human life. One of his first targets is the religious criticism of reason.

Paine notes that Christians tend to distrust and disparage reason in calling it "*human* reason." Christians are suspicious of reason because they believe it leads people away from God and religion rather than toward them. Paine, on the other hand, finds it ironic that Christians call reason "human." Human beings do not give reason to themselves. Reason is a gift from God. If reason is given to us by God, Paine's argument goes, then it is Godly reason and we ought to put it to good and proper use regarding religion.

Paine took issue with prayer, claiming it is ridiculous since it amounts to asking God to change the way things are. If the faithful believe that everything is as God wishes it to be, praying to change the way things are is absurd. Since Christians, according to Paine, hold the position that God knows best and has arranged the world so that it will be the best, Christians who pray to change what occurs are essentially saying that they know better than God what should happen.

Equally absurd is the Christian rejection of science. For Paine, science is not a human invention. Science comes from God since science is about the natural world and God is the creator of the natural world. So the methods we use to study, describe, and live within the natural world cannot possibly be inconsistent with truth about God. Science must be Godly and an activity more likely to give us truth about God than religion. The seasons change, sunlight makes plants grow, the air is fit to breathe – all these things, and more, indicate that there is a God who cares for us. The ultimate conclusion is that we are to be kind to each other in the same way that the God of nature is kind to us. If we are to live in a Godly way, then, we should have respect for science.

Christianity's doctrines are not consistent with the ultimate lesson from God that we are to be kind to each other. Christianity's ultimate teaching is murder (of Jesus). **Pecuniary justice** (Jesus paying for the sins of all humanity) takes the innocent for the guilty. We never intentionally or *rightly* allow an innocent person to suffer a penalty for the guilty. And we certainly should not celebrate the death of the innocent so that the evil may live.

Paine's view is that many of the claims of established religion are indefensible by reason and are simply not true. He rejected the **Trinity**, noting that it is obviously contradictory to believe that there can be three persons in one. He denied that Jesus voluntarily offered himself as a savior since in the story of the betrayal it is obvious that he was hiding and wished not to be found. Even though Paine did not mention Edwards by name, he claimed that beliefs like those of Edwards are a form of thanklessness to God insofar as Calvinist doctrines describe human beings as sordid, ulcerous, sinful, and unworthy of God's grace. For Paine, if we are

God's creation and God is good, it is unclear how it could be true that we have such lowly characteristics. In all, Paine's view is that the Christian lives a life of irreconcilable contradictions and that **Christianity** is not worthy of belief. Paine eschewed the veracity and quality of miracles, revelations, and prophecy, finding all of them to be irrational and contrary to a kind, good, powerful, all-knowing God. In one of his more humorous moments, Paine refers to the supposed miracle of Jonah and the whale, pointing out that it would be truly miraculous if Jonah had swallowed the whale rather than the other way around. Paine's position, put briefly, is that God is rational, not a God of wrath and fits of passion.

That Christianity is not worthy of Paine's belief, however, does not necessitate that belief in God is not justified. Paine was accused of being an atheist. His defense against charges of infidelity and **atheism** is that not believing in any God is atheism. Since he did believe in a God, he could not be an atheist. That Paine's position on the nature of God is different from that of Christians is unquestionable. That he did not believe in God is simply false.

Benjamin Franklin was drawn for a time to Deism but later returned to Christianity because Christianity offered more benefits than other religious doctrines he had considered. Jefferson, too, was drawn to Deism. He combined it with Christianity because, in his view, Jesus the person and Christianity the doctrine provided acceptable and functional moral guides. With respect to whether anyone must adhere to any religious doctrine at all, though, Jefferson's view is more Deistic than traditionally Christian. If we are capable of employing our rational faculty to discover truth, and if reason moves a person to a religion or away from it, that is the private business of that person. Just so long as the beliefs or creeds adopted or rejected do not harm others, we should be left free to believe or not to believe as we see fit.

While not hostile to Christianity or any other religious doctrine, there are elements of Franklin's position on religion that are similar to those of Paine and arise from the same reverence for reason. Franklin's thoughts on the utility of religion, proof for the existence of God, and the possibility of an afterlife appear in various forms in his *Autobiography* as well as in some essays and letters. Christian virtues are useful overall because they have benefits in this life. Avoiding slothfulness leads us away from indulgence and pain. Avoiding laziness is conducive to industry and profit. God's commandments are not what makes what they command good or what they forbid bad. God commands or forbids things because they are already good or bad. In addition, Jesus' divine status makes no difference to the moral teachings provided by his life and words. This view prefigures the attitude of the Pragmatists late in the eighteenth century who all considered it a waste of time and intellectual energy to try to answer questions that are unanswerable and that, even if they were answerable, would make no practical or concrete difference. If the moral teachings of Jesus and Christianity are worthwhile because they are useful, their source is irrelevant. Doctrines are true relative to us, relative to our needs, and justified by reason.

Even though Franklin and Paine agreed on the requirements of Enlightenment rationality, they did not agree on everything. Part of what it is to be the intellectual product of a time of free and unbridled inquiry is to find reasons for different positions. The problem of the determination of the will illustrates this. Where Franklin held that we are determined and that there is nothing evil in the universe, Paine argued against determinism and especially against the doctrine of predestination while agreeing with Franklin regarding the status of evil.

Franklin believed in predestination leading to theodicy. For Franklin, God is the first mover and creator of the universe. God is also **omniscient**, **omnibenevolent**, and **omnipotent**. So God is all knowing, all good, and all powerful so that what God knows is good, nothing can happen without God's consent, and there is no evil in the world. It makes no sense to claim that evil leads to a greater good since there is no greater good than what God does. If everything must be as it is and was created by God to be that way, all beings must be equal from God's point of view. Even though Franklin finds no reason to pray and believes that all beings are equally valued by God, he still holds out hope for an afterlife especially given the good fortune he has experienced in this world. It led him to believe that it will continue into the next life – even if it is undeserved.

Paine, on the other hand, found the doctrine of predestination nonsensical even though he agreed with Franklin that there may be an afterlife. Paine, however, believed that the afterlife must be earned. For Paine, if anything makes sense, it must be that God chooses for happiness in the next world those whose lives have been pure and good. So it must be that the doctrine of predestination is false.

Some people attribute to the revolutionary American founders claims that they never made. We have political pundits and half-baked entertainment news figures telling us that Thomas Jefferson was a devout Christian who never argued for the separation of Church and state, that Thomas Paine's views support libertarian positions on universal health care, and that all the Founders were Christians bent on ensuring that America begins and remains a Christian nation. That assessment of things, however, depends on what one means by "Christian" and whether one bothers to read and understand the history of the American republic. Jefferson once told Adams that he was a "real" Christian because he believed Jesus to be possessed of every human excellence. This statement includes nothing about worship, going to church, or establishing government on a "Christian" foundation.

Jefferson, being deeply entrenched in Enlightenment ideals regarding human autonomy and rationality, maintained that no one has the right to impose their beliefs on any other person and, indeed, that human beings are by right free not only to practice the religion of their choice but also to practice no religion at all. In the "Bill for Establishing Religious Freedom" in Virginia (1777), Jefferson argued it is a violation of **civil rights** for a state to force religion on its citizens and that it is ultimately contrary to the interests of the state to do so. Forcing people to adopt a belief or to claim that they adhere to a belief leads to hypocrisy and meanness. This Bill, which serves as the foundation of the First Amendment to the U.S. **Constitution**, provides specifically that no person may be forced to attend or participate in any place or practice of worship and that a person's choosing not to do so may not result in any penalties with respect to his freedom or his rights. How much more clear can it be that Thomas Jefferson did not argue that America was to become a Christian nation? That it was to be a moral nation, founded on the ideals of Enlightenment and consistent with the rights and dignity of humanity, is clear. That the Founders thought of Enlightenment reason as Godly is even more clear. But Enlightenment reason respects individual conscience and each person is to be left alone to worship (or not) as he sees fit.

Jefferson not only penned the document supporting freedom of and from religion, he lived the conclusion. He is not the only American to have looked with a skeptical eye on the Bible, but he is one of the few who took it upon himself actually to edit the Bible to make it read in a way he thought fully consistent with Christianity. Jefferson took sections of the Bible he held to be true, consistent, and fit for belief and put them into a volume of his own (*The Jefferson Bible*) that included only the sections of the Bible he thought indicative of true Christianity.

REVOLUTIONARY ETHICS, SOCIAL AND POLITICAL PHILOSOPHY

Franklin's position on ethics was simple and straightforward: it is up to individuals to create themselves and to be the best people they are capable of becoming. In "typical American" fashion, he set out to show how it could be done. Franklin embarked on a quest to become the "self-made man" that is distinctly and uniquely American. Franklin was not "every man" but he was his own person and this is what Enlightenment requires. Franklin set out to create a self using a method (which is thoroughly modern) to achieve perfection of moral character and action (Aristotelian and **virtue-theoretic**).

It is important that Franklin used a modern individualistic method of self-improvement to achieve the traditional ideal of excellence of character. There has been a general tendency in the history of American thought for people to divide themselves up into ideological camps, some taking a conservative approach to the function and nature of ethics and politics while others take a more liberal view. The liberal view conceives of us as self-interested, isolated, atomistic individuals. The conservative position is that we are "**encumbered**" **selves** who are thoroughly social beings. The liberal view makes it seem that people must be compelled to participate fully in the life of a community rather than to see themselves as natural participants in it. Note, for example, that the Hobbesian and Lockean stories of the formation of organized societies is informed by hypothetical individuals banding together in a natural condition not out of love or natural feelings of fellowship for each other but doing it because it is convenient and safer to do so than not.

On the other hand, a virtue-theoretic or **communitarian** view is more amenable to believing that we cooperate with each other and live in communities because we are naturally social beings with obligations to each other to live in productive communities. Whether it is the communitarian or the liberal, social relations revolve around productivity and communities in which productivity may be fostered. For the community-minded, productive and peaceful communities are built and maintained by the activity of individuals who have developed human excellences (virtues) that are beneficial to the community.

No matter one's preference for rugged individualism or for community, Franklin's approach to ethics is sure to be appealing. His commitment to the development of good moral character is consistent both with the needs and desires of community and with the Enlightenment's demand for rationality focused on the individual. Franklin has it both ways.

Franklin's project of self-creation is complex. It was his duty to create himself as the moral being he wished to become according to his understanding of Christian morality and because a citizen has an obligation to be the best and most productive person he is capable of becoming. The rational pursuit of self-perfection includes a list of 13 virtues such as temperance, silence, cleanliness, chastity, industry, and humility, among others. It is not so important what the virtues are as it is to see the manner in which he went about trying to instill them in himself, and what is philosophically significant about having given this project a try.

Franklin's project of self-creation and moral perfection goes well beyond a list of virtuous behaviors. It includes a method to assure that the virtues are attainable. Franklin determined that a week per virtue would be sufficient to make each one habitual, i.e., part of his character. Franklin's project springs from **virtue-ethics**. His method arises from modern and Enlightenment thought.

Virtue-ethicists consider people inseparable from communities. The function of community is to promote human happiness by promoting virtue in citizens while at the same time the virtue of the citizen helps to promote virtue in others and happiness in the community. It is a circle of causes, effects, and influences. It is thoroughly social. For virtue-ethics, the happiness and development of the individual are impossible without the influence and guidance of community because we are, at our core, social or political animals.

Seeing that virtue-ethics requires the influence of the community on the development of virtue, Franklin's self-improvement project, a "do it yourself" of virtue-ethics, is not fully consistent with either the form or the content of traditional virtue-ethics, but the intended consequences in Franklin's approach to virtue are essentially the same as that of other virtue-ethicists. Franklin used an individualistic and method-based approach to achieve the community's goal of creating the virtuously productive and ethically respectable individual. In this way, his project is both traditional and modern, it is conservative and liberal, all at once. Moreover, Franklin's project of self-perfection is **utilitarian** and, above all, pragmatic. Whether considering Franklin the self-made moral being or Franklin the entrepreneur and inventor or statesman, the question is always the same: What can I do?

Instead of counting on the community to tell Franklin what to be, what to do, how to act and what to become, he appealed to Enlightenment individual reason and embarked upon the project for the benefit of himself and the community. That he used a method in which he alone set the goals and set the procedures indicates more than a hint of respect for Enlightenment reason.

Revolutionary thinking covers science, religion, and ethics – and its influence in American politics affects the world. Understanding the thoughts and actions of the American revolutionary thinkers in this chapter is enhanced by understanding their intellectual heritage. American revolutionary thinkers used Enlightenment principles to argue against abuses of power and violations of rights perpetrated by the British government. They demonstrated the irrationality of illegitimate government power with reason, they argued against tyranny on the basis of human autonomy and dignity, and they claimed universal application of the truths of reason.

John Adams' view of the nature of humanity is similar to that of Hobbes in holding that people are self-interested and prone to disagreement and quarrel, especially in competitive conditions. For Hobbes, absolute government was the result of these facts of human nature. For Adams, arguing for division of powers in government was the result. Locke, who argued using a more gentle view of human nature in which people would be generally cooperative even without the benefit of a state, argued for limited government created by the people through their agreement. Paine agreed with Locke.

Adams maintained that people cannot be trusted always to do what is morally right and that private interests are likely to affect public action. As a result, we need to be careful in creating political structures and processes to protect the general happiness. Adams did not follow the Hobbesian lead and argue for absolute government but he also did not hold the more optimistic views of Locke, Jefferson, and Paine.

Paine thought most people were cooperative and reasonable but there is always lurking somewhere under the surface the potential to allow "wickedness" to overtake our generally good nature. Paine hoped for good nature to shine through but recognized political structures must take into account the actual behavior of human beings.

The need for government arises from self-interest and to ensure that individual rights are respected both by other individuals and governments. The political philosophy of the American revolutionaries, no less than their moral views, is more easily understood with a background in some of the formative ideas on which it depends.

Rights are at the center of the justification for the existence and power of government for Hobbes, Locke, Adams, Paine, and Jefferson. Since Hobbes and Locke provide the larger philosophical content for the arguments of the revolutionaries, it is to their positions on rights and freedom to which we now turn.

Hobbes' position is that there is one **natural right**. It is to defend oneself. It is consistent with the first and fundamental law of nature requiring us to defend and preserve our lives. For Hobbes, a right is a freedom and nature itself provides the freedom of self-defense through our native abilities; each of us is free to defend ourselves using whatever means we deem necessary. The right to defend oneself, however, is ineffective until enforced by the state. To combat this problem, Hobbes proposed that a significant function of government is to protect and ensure effective exercise of the right of self-defense.

According to Locke, we have God-given natural rights to life, liberty, and property. It is a matter of convenience and expediency to establish government to ensure that one's pursuits are made possible. Paine and Jefferson, both following Locke's lead, put emphasis on the right to revolt against a government that violates our rights. To violate one's rights is to violate human autonomy and dignity. In this, Adams also agreed. His view was that a representative government is conducive to the effective realization of dignity and the proper practice of morality and industry. Government's obligation to protect individual rights is useful and required by Enlightenment reason. For all of these thinkers except Hobbes, who nonetheless builds into his absolutist system of government the germ of the right to revolt, a government failing the test of usefulness or expediency in violating the rights of individuals offends individual dignity and ought to be replaced by a government more suitable and appropriate.

For all the revolutionaries considered in this chapter, a condition that government must satisfy is to limit laws and enlarge rights of citizens. Whether it is individuals, groups, or governments that interfere with the rights of individual people, it is always wrong for rights to be abridged or violated.

The importance and influence of Thomas Paine's revolutionary thinking about rights should not be underestimated. As the author of *Common Sense* (1776) and *The American Crisis* (1776–83), Paine argued against British rule and American subjection. In *The Rights of Man* (1791), Paine argued that rights belong to people by virtue of their humanity and only limited representative government is justified.

Paine argued that society exists prior to the formation of government. His view of the state of nature was that of cooperative individuals combining forces and abilities to satisfy human wants. Government would not be necessary if all people were governed by moral virtue. If they were, we could count on their continued cooperative activity. We cannot, however, trust people always to live up to the ideals of communal living. Like Locke's position on the issue, Paine contends that it is unfortunate but true that there are people who will not maintain moral and social control over themselves that would otherwise reasonably guarantee everyone free exercise and enjoyment of rights.

While individuals may not live up to their moral obligations, Paine does not resort to the position that government is the perfect solution to our problems. It is a "necessary evil" as the association of people to further their combined cooperative activity. In Paine's view of the natural condition, we already have rights and the function of government is to protect them. The rights we possess upon coming into the world are natural rights. The natural rights we are not able effectively to use, protect, and defend are ensured by government. The rights ensured by government are civil rights. Natural rights and civil rights are not, therefore, materially different from each other. They differ only because a civil right is a natural right that is "defective" in the individual so that civil rights are natural rights that the individual cannot effectively ensure or use on his own. It is important to note that government being necessary to secure rights does not imply that government *grants* rights to anyone. The individual has rights prior to the formation of government, some of which are effectively exercised by the individual. If government exists to protect rights, when government violates them it is no longer legitimate.

Jefferson championed the defense of individual rights. He was not so much interested in arguing for the *need for* government as he was in providing reasons *for revolution* arising from government's abuse of power. In the American Declaration of Independence, Jefferson did just that.

The most oft-quoted and well-known statement in American history is this:

> We hold these truths to be self-evident: that all men are created equal; that they are endowed by their creator with certain inherent and inalienable rights; that among these are life, liberty, & the pursuit of happiness: that to secure these rights governments are instituted among men, deriving their just powers from the consent of the governed.
> (American Declaration of Independence, 4 July 1776)

The statement is packed with implications.

To be "endowed by their creator with certain inherent and inalienable rights" is unambiguous if Jefferson was referring to the conception of rights like that of Locke or Paine, and there seems no compelling reason to think that Jefferson was not doing so. For Locke, natural and inalienable rights are given to us as gifts of God and there is no more justification needed. For Paine, respect for human dignity and autonomy leads necessarily to the same conclusion. Governments overstepping the bounds of power granted to them by the people are illegitimate and may be replaced. The people have a right to erect a new government that seems to them appropriate to achieve their rights to life, liberty, and the pursuit of happiness.

Paine trusted society generally but distrusted government specifically. For Paine, government must have only limited power. Adams distrusted society due to his Hobbesian view of human nature and argued for a government sufficient in structure and power to defeat rival claims of individual self-interest. Paine and Adams agreed that governments exist to protect rights.

Forming government to protect rights is inseparably tied to one's view of human nature and the nature of society. The formation of government is affected by the way in which (and whether) a constitution plays into government foundation. For Paine, a constitution forms a government, not the other way around. In *The Rights of Man* (1791), Paine asserts that a constitution is nothing more than the act of people creating a government. This means that people make an agreement with each other to form government and government is the result, but not a part of, the social contract. On this point, Paine and Hobbes agreed even though the ways in which and why governments are formed are considerably different. For Hobbes, because government is not part of the social contract, there is no sense in which government can violate any obligation specified in a constitution or social agreement. This means that injustice cannot be perpetrated by a sovereign on its people. Paine and Locke argued that government is part of the contract and *can* commit and be held accountable for injustices. The issue of the creation of a national constitution for the newly formed American republic was therefore both practically important and philosophically significant.

In "Thoughts on Government" (1776), Adams argued that direct democracy would be problematic. Adams argued instead for a division of powers to control the interests of factions and the influence of self-interest that would tend toward corruption in violating the rights of citizens. Adams' plan, which is the plan of Federalists, is division of powers in government to preserve liberty.

We must ask ourselves how the new American republic will operate most efficiently given self-interest as a major facet of human nature. What structures and procedures ought to be put in place to ensure that the new republic does not deteriorate and become autocratic? The answer to this question is not, as Paine would have it, that the people will be represented in a simple and direct fashion. Adams, in "A Defense of the Constitutions of the United States of America" (1787), contended that elected representatives cannot be trusted to protect the people's liberties because if they have all legislative, executive, and judicial power, they will violate the liberties of people even sooner than would an absolute **monarch**. It is erroneous to think that free people will not usurp others' rights because, Adams wryly noted, if it was true that people never think of violating the rights of others, there would be no need for government in the first place.

It is essential to divide powers of government to avoid the same pitfalls of human nature that affect the relationships between individual people: they are ruled by passions and are subject to disagreements. This is the reason that sovereign power cannot be entrusted to one assembly. For Adams, the majority and leaders will oppress the minority for their own benefit and to the detriment of the liberty and security of the minority.

For Adams the goal of government is the happiness of the people. Since the American revolutionaries did not seek to replace British autocracy with an equally oppressive American regime, an effective means to control self-interest is a separation of government powers where laws rule with a system of checks and balances.

Adams, like James Madison, was suspicious of direct democracy. Adams told Jefferson in a letter in 1815 that if we consult history we find that whenever the people are "unchecked" they are as bad or worse than any ruler with absolute power. It is then that the "**tyranny of the majority**" must be defeated. John Stuart Mill explained in *On Liberty* that the tyranny of society over individuals is worse than political oppression because it goes deep into individuals' personal lives. It is therefore essential to protect against the force of group opinion on the individual in addition to protecting against political tyranny. Something must be done to ensure that the new American republic does not suffer from the tyranny of the majority as a replacement for the tyranny of British rule.

James Madison took up where Adams left off on the issue of Federalism. Even though it may seem contrary to Adams' views on the dangers of **factions**, in "Federalist 10," Madison argues for the good that factions bring. Even if the interests of one group are dangerous to the interests of another, they are still part of what it is to live in a society in which freedom of thought and discussion are prized. In keeping with respect for freedom of speech, assembly, and conscience, Madison argued that it is much worse to try to control factions than it is to regulate their existence. Controlling factions limits liberties of individuals and, in practice, it is impossible to inculcate the same passions in all people. Furthermore, acceptable control of factions is possible with larger populations and larger geographic areas in which the population can live. If they are separated from each other, factions are unlikely to become very strong or have overwhelming influence on a majority of people.

Factions are completely controlled only when we remove their causes or remove their effects. Removing the causes of factions is worse than the "disease" of factions since it destroys individual liberty or gives to all people the same opinions, both of which are incompatible with individual liberty. Controlling the *effects* of factions is the only acceptable approach to the problem. It is achieved by representative government vested in different legislative, executive, and judicial branches. This solution enlarges liberty while at the same time protecting minority views and interests.

By properly controlling factions, division of power makes it less likely that people will try to rule over others in a hierarchy of human value. Instead, they will realize that laws ought to rule in a representative government. It is never safe to put all legislative, judicial, and executive power in one assembly. Countering Adams' pessimism about human nature, Madison expressed hope that even though self-interest is the factor driving human conduct, it will be controlled by virtue.

Madison seems to have been right that factions are controlled and their benefits can be realized, even if not perfectly, in the American republic. Where factions cannot and perhaps should not be controlled, the American revolutionaries built into the Constitution the ability, based on evolving and growing needs of the society and government to which the Constitution applies, to amend it. It is the way in which Jefferson's comment that "a little rebellion every now and then is a good thing" can manifest itself peacefully and codify changes that take place in a dynamic social and government system.

CRITICISMS OF REVOLUTIONARY THOUGHT

Enlightenment thinking is not perfect. There are **contradiction**s and inconsistencies deriving from it in practice. One of the results of Enlightenment thinking is that it led to the abuses and cruelty of the French Revolution. Another significant problem is that it continues, perhaps inadvertently, the tendency of past movements in philosophy and society toward absolutist thought. There remains the conviction among Enlightenment thinkers that there is "Truth" out "there" somewhere that is knowable by us, and that if we will only reason carefully we will find it.

Thomas Paine's criticisms of Christianity and other religious systems are filled with misrepresentations of the beliefs of actual practitioners of religious systems on the whole, including his apparent belief that all Christians are determinists and that the only thing for which Christians ever pray is to ask God to change the course of events. Where Franklin argued for determinism's ineluctable trek toward the conclusion that everything that exists is good, Paine questioned the very notion of determination of the will because he found it incompatible with God's goodness and the hope for eternal reward. Furthermore, Franklin's stance that everything in the world is good is obviously inconsistent with the fact of evil, hardship, pain, and suffering in the world. It seems very difficult to reconcile suffering – and especially **moral evil** caused by human beings – with the goodness of God. As William James pointed out over 100 years later, there are irreconcilable contradictions in belief in determination of the will and some new way of thinking about the issue is warranted.

The methods employed by Enlightenment thinkers and revolutionaries lead to varied conclusions about issues in metaphysics, epistemology, religion, ethics, and social and political thought that are incompatible with each other and that are therefore incommensurable. One particularly striking incompatibility in the thought of the American revolutionaries is manifested in the difference between the Federalists and **Anti–Federalists**. Anti-Federalists (such as Jefferson) believed that the central government formed by the U.S. Constitution was too strong and that the public good would be swallowed up in competing interests. Federalists tended to put too much emphasis on the notion that there is an essence of human nature leading to the need to control individual interests. On the other hand, it is perhaps one of the greatest strengths of the American experiment in representative government that it can accommodate a panoply of points of view and continue to thrive.

Even with the success of representative government in the United States, from the very beginning it has been characterized by differences in principles and policies that lead to impasse in making decisions or to lengthy processes allowing injustices to continue. One of those injustices is slavery which existed before, during, and after the period of the American Revolution and leaves an unpleasant legacy whose effects are yet to be resolved in American society and government.

In a letter to John Adams, Abigail Adams noted the inconsistency of American revolutionary ideas and actions in her comment that it is odd to fight for freedom while at the same time robbing freedom from slaves who have as much right to it as anyone else. She also implored her husband to "remember the ladies" in constructing the new American government. He did not. It is to the problem of slavery and the denial of rights and full citizenship to American women and African Americans that we turn in Chapter 4.

CONCLUSION

The American revolutionary thinkers of the eighteenth century replaced the dismal view of human nature and the impossibility of human improvement of the Calvinists with their own brand of optimism and reform. Even though there is a tendency in Enlightenment thinking to continue to seek absolute truth and absolute knowledge, the tendency did not extend to morality and government and even in some cases it did not extend in the metaphysical, epistemological, and religious realms. This is clear with the example of Franklin's **fallibilism**. Franklin explicitly said that we ought to indicate that the positions we take are tentative. This attitude is applicable overall to Enlightenment views in science, religion, and morality in that Enlightenment thinkers recognized that even if there is an ultimate truth "out there" in the universe, it may be that we are not equipped to grasp it. We ought, instead, to maintain a sense of intellectual humility in light of human frailty. The American revolutionaries and their ideas were far from perfect. That, however, does not keep American thought and American people from continuing to believe that there is always something better that they can achieve and do.

FURTHER READING

There are innumerable works on the American revolutionaries and their works. For introductory purposes, the following works are valuable: J. J. Ellis, *Founding Brothers: The Revolutionary Generation* (New York: Knopf, 2000); Morton White, *The Philosophy of the American Revolution* (New York: Oxford University Press, 1981); Pauline Maier, *American Scripture: Making the Declaration of Independence* (New York: Random House, 1997), Herbert J. Storing, *What the Anti-Federalists Were For: The Political Thought of the Opponents of the Constitution* (London: University of Chicago Press, 1981).

For Internet resources on the ideological basis of American revolutionary thought, see: *Digital History: Using New Technologies to Enhance Teaching and Research* at http://digitalhistory.uh.edu/database/article_display.cfm?HHID=263; *Documents from the Continental Congress and the Constitutional Convention*, 1774–89 at http://memory.loc.gov/ammem/collections/continental. See also American revolutionary documents and related resources at www.infidels.org, which has many original sources from Paine, Jefferson, and others.

4

BEYOND THE ENLIGHTENMENT REVOLUTIONARIES

RELIGION, ETHICS, AND SOCIAL AND POLITICAL PHILOSOPHY

The American revolutionaries made great strides in securing the promises of liberty, but they fell far short of doing so for all Americans. From the beginning of the new American republic, tension existed between ideals of liberty and equality and actual conditions in American society. The majority of African Americans were held as slaves, and women, no matter their race or color, were considered less than full citizens and were, like African Americans, often considered less than fully human. From the American Revolution to today, activism for reform has taken place to address the unrealized ideals of the founders.

Religion occupies a central place in applying the ideals and principles of American revolutionary thought to oppressed people. Religious conceptions provide part of the foundation required to argue for adequate changes to social structures that keep women and people of color from enjoying the benefits of American freedom and prevent them from being recognized by others (as well as sometimes by themselves) as possessors of dignity and value. Because the philosophical positions of the reformers of this chapter center on the use of religious concepts to address the moral, social, and political plight of slaves and women, the remainder of this chapter combines religious concepts and arguments in moral, social, and political realms.

THE PROBLEM OF SLAVERY

Just over a year before Jefferson wrote the Declaration of Independence (1776), Paine, ever the true revolutionary, wrote *African Slavery in America* (1775). The principles he put forth to defeat claims to the legitimacy of slavery are important and interesting for their moral strength. There is no sense in slaveholders justifiably claiming that they purchased slaves in a legitimate business transaction. The freedom of slaves has been stolen, and just as the owner of stolen property has a right to have it back regardless of how many times it has been sold to others, slaves are rightful owners of their freedom. That ancient Jews kept slaves did not move Paine. He noted that there are many things recorded in the Bible that are not fit to be imitated. Slavery is one of them. Paine's political argument makes transparent the inconsistency in the beliefs and actions of American colonists who held other people in bondage and complained that Britain enslaved them with unreasonable laws and taxes.

The only moral course of action was to free the slaves. Paine recognized that the British might offer slaves freedom in return for loyalty, making slaves dangerous to American colonists. To avoid this problem and gain benefit for the colonists, Paine proposed giving freed slaves settlements on the Western frontiers.

Jefferson argued in favor of emancipation, but with a decidedly ugly turn. In *Notes on the State of Virginia* (1781) Jefferson made blatantly racist and surprisingly unscientific claims regarding African American intelligence, morality, physical characteristics, and abilities. Despite unsavory comments, Jefferson favored emancipation, but it was not emancipation *and* full participation in American society and government. It was emancipation and *expatriation*. Jefferson argued that sending freed slaves to Africa was necessary because it would be impossible for white former slave-holders and freed African Americans to live in the same geographical region due to the abuses that the latter suffered at the hands of the former. In other words, Jefferson's solution to the problem of wrongs suffered by slaves was to commit *more* wrongs against them.

While Jefferson and Paine offer some hope for emancipation, their arguments are suspect. Even while offering moral arguments against slavery, Paine apparently could not resist finding benefit for white people in providing defense for white colonists. Jefferson's arguments have little moral or social value. The intellectual and moral conflict in Jefferson's arguments are blatant given his ideals for human rights in the Declaration of Independence and the fact that he claimed ownership of over 200 human beings. So while Jefferson was in principle a champion of individual rights and dignity for all human beings, his commitment to rights and principles consistent with dignity was applied inconsistently.

The tension between American ideals and actions with respect to slavery represents an uncomfortable contradiction in American society that did not diminish for many years. It continued nearly unabated throughout the first half of the nineteenth century, and even after the Civil War and the legal emancipation of slaves, African Americans were treated by the U.S. government and most Americans in the North and South as only second-class citizens at best. They were regularly treated with nearly indescribable cruelty and injustice, and in the "Jim Crow" South after the Civil War, laws were passed effectively criminalizing the exercise of civil rights by African Americans.

In contrast to early arguments against slavery, Richard Furman (1755–1825) and Thomas Dew (1802–46) employed scriptural arguments for the institution of slavery. Furman, a South Carolina Baptist preacher, wrote a letter to the governor of South Carolina in 1823 offering a two-part argument against emancipation and for the "morality" of slavery. Contrary to Paine, Furman held that God commanded the Jews to take slaves. On the other hand, Furman contended that humane treatment of slaves is required by morality and that slavery ought not to be associated with cruelty.

"Moral" arguments Furman used to justify slavery are grounded in utilitarian and virtue-theoretic considerations. Like Jefferson, Furman believed that slaves were ignorant and dominated by "passion." Being ruled by passion renders a person incapable of moral freedom (since that requires reason) and therefore incapable of political freedom. He concluded it best to keep African Americans as slaves since they will be "happier" that way. Second, freeing slaves would injure the community. Furman did not explain the "injury" that would result, but he did note that freeing slaves into a condition in which both they and the community would be disadvantaged could not possibly be required. An additional argument centered on **benevolence** using twisted virtue-ethics reasoning is that if benevolent actions are virtuous only when done freely, then to *require* benevolence abrogates freedom. His bizarre analogy makes the point that even though it is generous for a person to release debtors from debts, it is not *required* that one benefit others. In similar fashion, even if it were an act of benevolence to release slaves, it is not truly an act of benevolence, and hence not moral, if slave-holders are *forced* to do so.

What Richard Furman ignored is that even if slave-holders treat slaves without physical cruelty, there is certainly cruelty in limiting freedoms and rights of human beings. The solution to slaves' ignorance is education, not more ignorance; and the solution to problems of disadvantage is to solve them, not to sweep them under the rug of slavery and act as though justice has been done in arguing for the better treatment of people held in bondage and abject conditions. Furman did not entertain the notion that emancipation is simply the right thing to do. He also focused his attention solely on the moral implications of emancipation for white slave-holders, ignoring the moral implications of emancipation for slaves.

It is beyond question that Furman's "benevolence" argument is absurd. While it is reasonable to claim that acts of benevolence are not truly benevolent when they are forced, to compare the lives of African American slaves to pieces of real property that might be sold and the proceeds distributed to the poor is to hold that African Americans are not considered human and have no moral standing at all. Furman's analogy to property simply does not hold. Liquidating property and distributing proceeds to benefit other people does no injustice to a piece of material property. In being freed, the slave benefits *as a human being*. His freedom is not a matter of benevolence *to* others, but it is a matter of *right* for the slave.

In *The Pro-Slavery Argument* (1853), Thomas Dew argued that slavery is beneficial to republican equality since white citizens in the South thought of themselves as equal due to the notice they take of their own freedom and the inferiority of African American slaves. Dew's reasoning is truly despicable and twisted, illustrating the lengths to which proponents of the institution of slavery go to justify its existence and to affirm the superiority of white European

Americans. Dew's focus on the reason white people think of themselves as equals in the South is bizarre. The argument proceeds on the notion that in the South, all white people consider themselves equal to each other. In other words, white people think of each other in the republican spirit of equality as moral and social equals and are facilitated in that belief by comparing themselves to the abject position of slaves who, by their condition, inadvertently offer white Americans a feeling of superiority over African Americans that translates into a feeling of equality among white Americans. The feeling of equality for white Southerners is all, in short, at the expense of African Americans.

In opposition to attempts to argue that slavery is morally justified, abolitionists used a variety of legitimate moral and political arguments. William Lloyd Garrison (1805–79), in "Declaration of Sentiments of the American Anti-Slavery Convention" (1833), appealed to the Declaration of Independence, believing that it justified abolition of slavery. He argued that the plight of slaves was immeasurably worse than the conditions of British subjects prior to the American Revolution. While the colonists had legitimate grievances against the British, they were never slaves.

While using the Declaration of Independence as the moral foundation for anti-slavery arguments, Garrison rejected the U.S. Constitution because it included the infamous "**three-fifths**" **clause** in which slaves each counted as only 60 percent of a person. This method of "counting" human beings negated freedom, reduced dignity, and denied the full humanity of African Americans. The Constitution, therefore, lacks moral force because it includes *restriction* or *denial* of rights of some people while the Declaration of Independence *affirms* the rights of all human beings. Abolition is consistent with the Declaration in restoring the human being to himself. Slavery and the Constitution deny the human being his rights.

Frederick Douglass, in "What to the Slave is the 4th of July" (1852), contended that there is nothing for the slave to celebrate regarding the 4th of July. Douglass refused to celebrate the holiday because, as a former slave, to celebrate the independence of American people from British oppression was obviously traitorous to the ideals on which the country was founded. The conflict between ideals of liberty and the practice of holding human beings in bondage obviates the need to *argue* that slavery is wrong. We know that it is false to claim that slavery is justified since the claim that freedom is the ideal of America is true. The document the holiday is meant to honor is not being used properly, or appropriately respected, when it can exist side-by-side with slavery.

Douglass' position is that slaves are human beings and, hence, moral beings. Moral beings are intellectual and responsible beings. Every human being has property in his own body and slavery denies the slave rightful ownership of his own body. All anyone really needs to do is to consider himself in slavery, and he will know that it is wrong for him. If it is wrong for any human being, it is wrong for all.

Garrison and Douglass both argued from a contractarian, natural rights approach affirming the humanity, and hence the equal rights, of African Americans. Angelina Grimké, however, provided a different kind of argument in *An Appeal to the Christian Women of the South* (1836) in which she used a Kantian argument for the obligation of white Southern American women to work toward the emancipation of slaves. It is the duty of Southern women to work for abolition by arguing against slavery, to free those they held, or to help slaves to escape. Any consequences befalling women or the slaves are not relevant to the morality of action and the moral responsibility to free enslaved human beings. Grimké's argument appeals to the universality of the principle guiding one's actions and the conception of "respect for persons" that is central to the moral system of Immanuel Kant. In this, it is simply right to work toward the emancipation of slaves. It is the right, and not the good, that ultimately matters for Angelina Grimké and Immanuel Kant.

Angelina Grimké's moral arguments against slavery and the duty of Southern American women to work toward the emancipation of slaves are **deontological**, formulated to stress the universal requirement to end slavery and the "respect for persons" aspect of the Kantian categorical imperative, the ultimate rule of Kantian **deontology** expressed in the notion that it is necessary always to treat human beings as an end only and never merely as a means to an end. There is no reasonable person who can deny that African Americans are human. Grimké noted the irony in slave-holders often using the term "**chattels personal**" to refer to slaves. Using that term allowed slave-holders to believe they were justified in paying slaves no wages for work. In the same way that one does not pay an ox for plowing a field, one who has no more regard for a slave than for an ox will feel justified in exploiting their labor.

As part of her argument for emancipation, Grimké also argued for the education of slaves. It is much easier to hold a person in slavery when the person is kept in ignorance. One who does not know that he has rights will not insist upon exercising them, and those who rob others of their rights can do so only by reducing the slave to the status of a thing. Education is therefore the key to freedom. It is the duty of Southern women (and indeed it is the duty of all human beings) to do what they can to educate slaves and to continue educating African Americans once they are free.

It is important also that Angelina Grimké's sister, Sarah, in "Letter VIII. On The Condition of Women in the United States" (1837) specifically lamented the plight of one class of women in America who were subject to the most grievous, gross, and inhumane treatment. She noted the unforgivable injustices suffered by female slaves at the hands of their purported owners, but she did not stop there to put the blame solely on Southern men. She noted that white women may benefit from the barbarous treatment of slave women by not being the target of it themselves. To acquiesce in injustice for one's own benefit is no excuse for sitting idly by and allowing injustice to go unchallenged.

Slavery finally ended with the **Emancipation Proclamation** of 1863 and the complete abolition of slavery in the United States by the end of the Civil War in 1865. Unfortunately, however, African Americans were to face additional personal and social barriers in attempting to achieve full political participation, to be afforded respect as human beings, and to be able effectively to exercise their rights as citizens. Many of the struggles African Americans faced prior to and immediately after the American Civil War continue today.

AMERICAN WOMEN'S RIGHTS

For both African Americans and American women, the road to recognition of moral, social, and legal equality was – and continues to be – long and arduous. Prior to **woman suffrage**, unmarried American women could hold and own property, but they were regularly denied the right to keep it upon marriage. They were subject to laws but not fairly represented by them. American women who held property were subject to taxation while at the same time denied the right to vote. In other words, they were taxed without representation or full participation in the political process. American women were almost always excluded from educational opportunities (as were most African American men) like those made available to white males simply on the basis of the fact that they were women.

Even though there were many women who wrote and spoke on women's rights and suffrage prior to and after the American Civil War, the works of Sarah Grimké (1792–1873) and Elizabeth Cady Stanton (1815–1902) are particularly valuable for their philosophical merit.

Sarah Grimké argued for the rights and dignity of human beings from a theological and moral foundation. She argued for the *equality* of men and women. Her arguments centered on God's intent in Creation, the moral obligations of human beings, and the intellectual capacity possessed by both sexes. The equality of which she wrote was religious, moral, and intellectual.

In "Letter I. The Original Equality of Woman" (1837), Sarah Grimké did not argue for the morally *laudable* equality of men and women. She instead argued for the equal *culpability* of male and female by denying the common interpretation of the fall from grace. On that view, Eve committed a moral wrong and Adam was her victim. Sarah Grimké, however, was not convinced that the traditional, common interpretation is accurate. In her reading, Adam was just as responsible for the fall from grace as Eve (so they are equal in moral standing), and in fact she said she would feel much more likely to agree that men are morally superior to women if Adam had done something to stop Eve rather than sharing in her guilt. Adam does not, therefore, stand as a moral exemplar in the story of the fall from grace.

Grimké expands further in "Letter IV. Social Intercourse of the Sexes" (1837) on the notion that social convention supports male and female inequality. Put plainly, the social meetings of men and women ignore the moral value and dignity of both and instead lead them to focus on sexual activity and gratification. Her wish is that men and women begin to recognize each other instead as companions in morality.

Biblical and duty-based arguments for women's rights like those of Sarah Grimké were soon to be eclipsed by the more secular and often much more caustic words and actions of Elizabeth Cady Stanton, *the* philosopher of the early American woman's rights movement. Stanton was co-organizer of the first (ever) woman's rights convention held in 1848 in Seneca Falls, New York.

Stanton's work involves and capitalizes upon knowledge of the philosophy of the American Revolution in the Declaration of Independence. It echoes and extends the Emersonian brief for self-reliance in her 1892 speech, "The Solitude of Self." She expressed the ways in which women are oppressed with vehement passion in her groundbreaking work, *The Woman's Bible* (1895, 1898). It is to these three works that we will turn our attention since they represent her contributions to the philosophy of religion, ethics, and political thought with arguments for sustained action to realize the promise of American freedom for women.

Stanton's speech at the convention in 1848 was considered, even by supporters, to be revolutionary and dangerous. She outlined the list of grievances of American colonists of 1776 to highlight their similarity with the grievances women continued to have against men and why women ought to assert their rights just as the colonists had done. Among women's grievances were tyrannical rule by government and society. Women were taxed on property and had no right to vote, they lost property upon marriage, and a woman became the property of her husband upon marriage. Women were therefore rendered civilly dead and any of their interests was supposed, usually wrongly, to be represented by the votes and political activity of their husbands.

The moral, social, and political conditions of women were unacceptable because they were contrary to the Enlightenment ideals of self-government, the promises of the social contract, and the human capacities and experiences of women. The Enlightenment revolutionaries argued that it is the natural right of every person to determine the government under which he (or she, for Stanton) will live and to have a voice in making laws, rules, and procedures. When women are denied the right to vote, it is another way in which men continue to enact laws and strengthen social conventions to create and sustain injustices against women.

For Stanton, one of the main stumbling blocks in the way of women taking their rightful place as full citizens – and indeed as complete human beings – was the Bible. In her view, the Bible did nothing to dignify women and served as the vehicle by which men could continue to force women into positions of sub-ordination, subservience, and ignorance. *The Woman's Bible* was written by Stanton and some of her intellectual cohorts (among them Biblical scholars) who were courageous enough to *edit and comment* on the Bible. Stanton was undeterred by friends who refused to participate or by vague threats that she or they would be ridiculed for the audacity of women to undertake the task. She saw it as no more odd for women to edit and comment on the Bible than it was for revising committees put in place by ecclesiastical authorities to edit the Bible and, in doing so, ensure that their interests were well represented. It should be no different for women.

Of the considerable number of biblical passages to which Stanton and her co-editors refer in *The Woman's Bible*, some of the most phi-losophically important are arguments against depictions of women as morally immature and incapable of self-government. Stanton rejected the biblical contention that women are rightly subject to men because a woman is at fault for the fall from grace. Stanton elevates the status of Eve rather than assigning blame to her. As some commentators have noted, Eve was interested in gaining knowledge *as a rational and intellectual being* and therefore she was certainly not rightly subject to domination and subordination by Adam. She was seeking knowledge; Adam was not.

Stanton notes that in Exodus ii, reference exists to few women and even fewer are actually named. Although Stanton did not discuss it, mention or remembrance of a person's name is a sign of respect. But women, in the Bible often unnamed and in Stanton's time identified by their husband's names, were afforded lower status than men. A clear indication of a woman's identity being swallowed up in that of her husband is to refer to her as "Mrs. John Smith" rather than to use her given name. Keeping one's name is an expression of self-respect and a way in which to signify that a woman is not the property of – nor is she subsumed literally under the name of – a husband. Many other injustices too numerous to mention here are evidence enough that the woman's status, whether in scripture or in law, whether in the time of Moses or in the late nineteenth century, was lower than that of men.

Stanton and her co-editors attempted to show that men and women are moral equals also by adopting an alternate **account of Creation** found in Genesis. In it, Adam and Eve were created together rather than separately from each other. In one account, man and woman are said to have been created at the same time and are therefore, in Stanton's view, equal to each other. The second view is that woman was created from the rib of Adam (and he named her, giving him dominion over her just as he named the animals and had dominion over them), and that she was created later made her inferior to him. In Stanton's reasoning, however, to believe that the second account of Creation (woman created later than man) is the true and accurate one necessitates that one admit men to be inferior to other animals since man was created *after* them. For Stanton, the reasoning used to "prove" the inferiority of women is not merely bad, it is severely mistaken.

The purpose of *The Woman's Bible* was at least two-fold. First, it served to make evident parts of the Bible that depict women negatively. Second, it was an overtly revolutionary action by Stanton to demand that women's interests and rights be taken into account. In part to support claims to the equality of women with men, Stanton proposed a theory of a matriarchy in "The Matriarchate, or Mother-Age" (1891), a position that gained popularity among some early **feminists**. The **matriarchate** is the belief that there was a historical time in which women ruled entire societies and, if we were either to return to this arrangement of rule or at least shared rule between men and women (the latter was Stanton's preference and the condition she predicted was close at hand, called the **amphiarchate**), society would be much improved. Mothers' influence in the public sphere would create a society in which ignorance, poverty, crime, war, and social ills would no longer exist. Under **patriarchy**, all of these social and political problems run rampant, and as patriarchy seems impotent to solve them, the example and rule of mothers may lead to benefits for everyone.

In "Solitude of Self," Stanton argued that women must not be dependent upon men and must be treated in ways consistent with maturity as a rational being. Stanton pointed out that people tend to not see that lonely and pervasive "solitude of self" is inescapable. Part of human maturity and dignity is to recognize the right of "**self-sovereignty**." Stanton's view was that humans are solitary islands of rights-possession and dignity who happen to be part of a community. She shares this position with a very significant number of theorists in the history of American philosophy and, indeed, throughout the history of Western thought. She maintained that the individual must recognize for herself what is true and not be led by the chains of authority and tradition to remain silent and powerless in the course of her life. It is the duty of the human being to speak, learn, and live for herself. Anyone depriving her of this right creates injustice and commits unconscionable moral error.

Men in the nineteenth century had access to educational opportunities that were simply unavailable to women. The prevailing attitude was that women had no need of higher education because their primary occupation was in the home. As a result, education for women was not unheard of, but it was usually not equal to that of men in content or availability. To argue for the need for women to be well-educated and for their rights to be respected, Stanton argued in "Solitude of Self" that each person is ultimately alone in solving most problems. It is consistent with the rights and interests of each person to be able to face and overcome overwhelming fear that sometimes confronts us in the most difficult and trying times. A woman (or man) without the good fortune to become well-educated, however, lacks the capacity needed to fight loneliness, frustration, and paralyzing fear that ignorance and loneliness involve.

There are several competing views of the meaning of Stanton's work on self-sovereignty. One is that people must be prepared to live with, to fight for, and to suffer by themselves. But women are not well-prepared to face challenges due to widespread conventional wisdom that women have husbands, brothers, or other male protectors who will share her problems or solve them for her. Stanton argued, however, for education sufficient to allow women the opportunity to exercise their right as autonomous and rational moral agents to solve their own problems. Another interpretation of "self-sovereignty" is the right of women to control their sexual lives. It is certainly not out of the question to take this interpretation as an *implication* of "Solitude of Self" in that self-sovereignty must include the right to determine for oneself, unimpeded by the opinions or actions of others, what one will do with or allow to happen in and to one's own body. A third view of "self-sovereignty" is that it is an overarching statement of the universal need of all people to stand on their own and to determine the course of their lives. While these are reasonable inferences from the text of "Solitude of Self," they seem incomplete. I offer a fourth view arising from the standpoint from which Elizabeth Cady Stanton argued for the rights and dignity of women. The foundation of her argument is derived from a modernist and Enlightenment conception of the autonomy and rationality of the individual human being in a contractarian moral, social, and political framework. Stanton argued that full participation in moral, social, and political spheres requires individuals to be responsible for the direction of their lives. To be deprived of choices is oppression. To be subject to a law and not to have a say in creating or applying it renders people little more than children incapable of deciding for and ruling over themselves. Stanton notes in *The Woman's Bible* that many women are comfortable at home with a strong man on whom to lean. Unfortunately, however, good husbands occasionally die and leave the family without a protector. In emergencies like this, the independent, strong, and educated woman will be able to survive. Stanton's exhortation to every person to achieve self-sovereignty is a way in which the individual can assert natural rights and individual dignity. It is also a call to recognize the need of all American citizens for education not simply to face the difficulties of this life alone, but to be able to participate as equals in American society. American citizens vote alone (each vote counts as one, and each person counts as one), each seeks the good for herself or himself, and anyone who violates rights violates the requirements of Enlightenment thinking that each person is the central point of authorization of power and the guarantor of truth in moral, religious, social, and political realms.

There are people in twenty-first-century America who think that women and men are now moral and political equals and that discussions of what happened in the past are no longer relevant to individuals or to society. This view, however, is mistaken. In many parts of the world today, women are treated as property, their individual interests and rights are subordinated to groups or to the interests of others, and they are disrespected in myriad ways. Political attacks on women's reproductive rights are an indication that many of the injustices to which the early American civil rights and women's rights activists turned their attention well over a century ago remain applicable today.

CRITICISMS

Jefferson's statements regarding characteristics of African Americans are simply false. While his contention that slavery ought to be abolished is on its face laudable, expatriation as the solution to the "problem" of emancipated people leaves much to be desired. Paine argued to abolish slavery because African Americans have rights that are not to be violated by anyone for any reason. On the other hand, he argued for the use value of freed slaves in protecting the frontier and property of white Americans rather than arguing for the value that each freed human being has in herself or himself.

The arguments of Dew and Furman are simply absurd. It is disturbing that so many people accepted "justifications" from the Bible and social convention largely without question. Fortunately for the history of American philosophy, for American society, and especially for African Americans, the institution of slavery found detractors whose voices and arguments meant to effect positive moral, social, and political change would not be silenced.

Angelina Grimké's arguments against slavery, while laudable in principle and consistent with the ethical theory she adopted, are problematic at some points. Her argument for the duty of Southern women to free slaves relies more on obligations to God than it does to African Americans who have a right to be free simply because they are human beings. Her argument rests instead on obligations human beings have to *God* to free and educate slaves. Even though Grimké's arguments are certainly meant to be effective in the fight against slavery, they do little to encourage respect for African Americans as human beings.

Regardless of the fact that most American citizens prior to the Civil War subscribed to some sect of Christianity, Angelina Grimké's argument applies only to Christians (even if the deontological elements of the argument extend to the obligations of all human beings). Her arguments may not translate well into the requirements of other religions, or to the requirements of atheists or agnostics to heed the call to action against slavery.

On the equality of the sexes, Sarah Grimké's argument turns on the problem of gender. She argued that God obligates us to recognize each other as moral and rational beings, not as beings possessed of gender or sexual differences. It would not have been significant in her time, but it certainly is in ours, that the attempt to "de-sex" or "de-gender" human beings does them no service in arguing for moral equality or equal status. The individual, moral, social, and political existences of men and women are largely shaped by bodily conditions.

Garrison's position is weakened considerably by not taking advantage of the legal status of the U.S. Constitution to argue for the equal status of African Americans with white citizens. Significantly, it is in the Constitution that the freedom and rights of African Americans (and all people) may be affirmed. Garrison's position downplays the legal requirements of the Constitution and affirms the moral rights of the Declaration of Independence. It is not that Garrison's use of the Declaration of Independence to argue for abolition of slavery rendered his arguments ineffective or irrelevant, but using a moral argument to create a legal and social condition (the abolition of slavery) while discounting the document in which a change in legal and social status of African Americans could begin to take place weakens the force of Garrison's claims.

Elizabeth Cady Stanton stands out for clarity of argumentation and the wide ranging spheres in which the social inferiority of women can be challenged. On the other hand, some of Stanton's arguments are strained and exaggerated. Her claim that the matriarchate would solve all social problems is perhaps an important possibility, but there is little evidence of a significant number of peaceful or long-standing matriarchal societies. Even if many had existed, Stanton's arguments for the equality of women with men contradict the claim that women would necessarily provide *better* structure and a more peaceful social and political existence as leaders of whole societies. Alternately, however, Stanton's implication that the experiences of women in the moral and social realms are different from those of men, and so their views of morality and the proper organization of society are also different, is like an ethics of care approach to moral reasoning that we will see in Chapter 8. Even though some of her arguments were off-base, erroneous, or exaggerated, her work stands as an important quest for appropriate recognition of the rights and dignity of women.

CONCLUSION

The work of American reformers for abolition and for women's rights is consistent with tendencies in American philosophy to focus on revolution and change, the practical application of philosophical positions, and securing freedom, rights, and justice for women and African Americans. It is largely a continuation of the American Revolution's philosophy of freedom.

The focus on practical application of the thought of the continuing revolutionaries is embodied in the use and good to which their arguments could be put. America could not continue to hold African Americans and American women in low moral, social, and political positions because doing so is inconsistent with the principles upon which the American republic was founded. In the next chapter, a different sort of continuation of the thought and ideals of the American Revolution takes place with the New England Transcendentalists, in the African American philosophy of W. E. B. Du Bois, and in the anarchism of Emma Goldman.

FURTHER READING

On abolitionist argument and action, see Mark E. Brandon, *Free in the World: American Slavery and Constitutional Failure* (Princeton, NJ: Princeton University Press, 1998) and Gerda Lerner's *The Grimké Sisters from South Carolina* (New York: Oxford University Press, 1998).

For early American women's rights, see Lois W. Banner, *Elizabeth Cady Stanton: A Radical for Women's Rights* (Boston: Longman, 1997); Beth Waggenspack, *The Search for Self-Sovereignty* (Westport, CT: Greenwood, 1989); and Kathryn Kish Sklar, *Women's Rights Emerge Within the Anti-Slavery Movement, 1830–1897: A Brief History with Documents* (Boston: St. Martin's, 2000).

5

NEW ENGLAND TRANSCENDENTALISM AND THE CONTINUING SPIRIT OF REFORM

The primary spokesmen for New England Transcendentalism are Ralph Waldo Emerson (1803–82) and Henry David Thoreau (1817–62). Their philosophy is in part a variation on Kantian metaphysics and epistemology and it is meant to transform Americans and American culture. Much like the revolutionary women and Abolitionists who were their contemporaries, the New England Transcendentalists speculated and wrote about issues and events having significant effects on moral, social, and political life. In "Resistance to Civil Government" (1849), Thoreau directly addressed the injustice of the Mexican-American War and the atrocious treatment of runaway slaves in a country ironically priding itself for championing liberty, equality, and dignity for all. Thoreau offered a means to combat injustices that he thought would cut them off at their base if only more people would speak and act against them. The Transcendentalists expected those who theorized about the independence, freedom, fairness, uniqueness, and power of America to put their words into practice.

Emerson and Thoreau encouraged Americans to become uniquely American not only in principle but also in fact and deed. Whether it is Emerson extolling the virtues of virile action to become uniquely American or Thoreau living a deliberate and solitary life at Walden Pond, the message is the same: to realize in oneself and in one's society the capacity for unique self-creation to transform social and political life to fit the dignity and value of the human being.

That one must become truly and uniquely oneself and that Americans must become truly and uniquely American find expression in Emerson's "Self-Reliance" (1841) and "The American Scholar" (1837). Further, the requirement of each person not to be spineless and cowardly is in Thoreau's *Walden* (1854) and "Resistance to Civil Government" (1849).

The grand expression of human possibility in the works of Emerson and Thoreau has affinities to Kantian ethics in the moral imperative to treat human beings always as ends in themselves, and also to Friedrich Nietzsche on the person of power and dignity as an **"Over-Man"** or **"Übermensch"** in building an ideal society. The germ of Nietzsche's Übermensch is found in Emerson and Thoreau and is expressed by Nietzsche in "Thus Spoke Zarathustra" (1883) and in *On the Genealogy of Morals* (1887) in which Nietzsche gave a compelling account of the reasons so many human beings do not reach this level of human attainment.

Kant insisted that every human being having the capacity to give the moral law to himself entitles rational beings to respect. No rational human being requires being told how to live his life or what to do. The rational human being is an end in himself. Nietzsche recognized something similar to the Kantian requirement that ends in themselves being treated with dignity and honor in his criticism of the blandly ordinary and pathetic tendencies of people to follow the crowd rather than to forge their own way in the world. Exerting one's individuality and strength is the Nietzschean **Will to Power**. While "Will to Power" is a term used by neither Emerson nor Thoreau, what they express is strikingly similar to what Nietzsche put forth several decades later.

The works and ideas of Emerson and Thoreau are excellent examples of the tendency among many American philosophers to focus on revolution, transforming ways of living and being, and attending to social issues to create moral progress. Their works center on why it is important to recognize the dignity and value of the individual human being to forge social change. The intent of both Emerson and Thoreau was that people adopt Transcendentalism as a way of life to transform self and society. The transformation is to live a truly dignified human life of respect for self and others by living as autonomous agents in a society of strength and true independence to change a world demanding conformity and banality. Thoreau notes that people often tell Americans that they are intellectually stunted compared with ancient Greeks and Elizabethans. Thoreau, however, replied that if someone is a pygmy he should not despair over it; he should instead strive to be the biggest pygmy he is capable of becoming.

TRANSCENDENTALIST METAPHYSICS AND EPISTEMOLOGY

For Emerson, feeling and intuition are much more important than reason and observation in acquiring knowledge. Feeling and intuition, constituting what Emerson calls "**Reason**," are distinct from external rationality and observation, which are merely "**Understanding**." Feeling/Reason will lead to knowledge of what is ultimately real. Emerson's terminology is strained, but the bulk of the position is derived from his attempt to use Kant's metaphysics in stating Transcendentalist ideals.

Much work has been done in the history of American philosophy on Emerson's indebtedness to – and misunderstanding of – Kant's metaphysics, but a brief statement of the distinction between Kant's metaphysics and Emerson's use of it will be sufficient to understand Emerson's stand on the divinity of humanity in transcending this worldly experience. It is equally important and useful in understanding Emerson's religious, moral, social, and political views.

Kant's metaphysics and epistemology derived from his reading of David Hume. Hume showed that the convictions that cause and effect relationships and the principle of nature's uniformity are not objects of knowledge because they are not known with absolute certainty and they are not verifiable in human experience. Cause and effect relationships are merely intellectual habits of the mind resulting from observation of ordered pairs or the psychological expectation that what has occurred in the past will continue into the future. The "**principle of nature's uniformity**" cannot be proven to be an object of knowledge. Trying to show that it is results in circular reasoning. We contend that we "know" that the future will resemble the past because it has always been that way.

But the assumption that it has "always" been that way is exactly the point in question.

Hume was a skeptic and empiricist who affirmed that all ideas arise from sense experience and that knowledge is of two kinds: rational ("**relations of ideas**") and experiential ("**matters of fact**"). Relations of ideas are necessary truths. Kant called necessary truths "**a priori**" because they are not dependent upon experience. Matters of fact, however, are truths whose denials are possible, i.e., their denials are not logically contradictory. The "**a posteriori**" are experiential truths derived from past and present experience.

The implications of Hume's epistemology led Kant to build a new conception of knowledge. Kant claimed that we come into the world with the ability to organize experience according to "categories of the understanding." Experience is organized through native capacity, an example of which is to think in terms of cause and effect relationships. If we come into the world with intellectual structures allowing us to organize experience, we *create* experience. The result is inability to know the "real essence" of external things. The terms used by Kant to distinguish between the world of appearances and the reality outside perception are "**phenomena**" and "**noumena**," respectively. For Kant, if we cannot know the true nature of the external world, it was necessary to show what it is about *us* that makes knowledge of the external world impossible. The realm of things as they are transcends the limits of knowledge. While we are confident that the noumena exist, we have no access to them. Instead, we bring organizational principles to experience.

Emerson adopted a variation on Kant's metaphysics and epistemology. Whether he misunderstood Kant's work and this led to his variation on Kantianism is not relevant to our purpose. What matters is what Emerson did with the distinction between Reason and the Understanding and what this has to do with knowledge, religious belief and practice, and human moral and social existence.

Emerson said we are capable of understanding things as they are if we will only transcend the limitations of sense experience through feeling and intuition. This, for Emerson, is "Reason." Because we are God-like, we have the capacity to transcend this–worldly experience to know the reality behind mere appearances. Appearances and experience give us "Understanding." Understanding (roughly equivalent to Kant's phenomena) is sufficient for simply getting by in the world. But to attain true comprehension of the nature of things requires that we go beyond mere appearances through a mystical experience providing knowledge of reality. This Emersonian view of the nature of both "Reason" and "Understanding" is clearly not the same as the Kantian distinction indicating that experience of reality external to the knower is impossible since it is the noumenal world to which we have no access as beings trapped in the phenomenal world.

The upshot of Emerson's position on the nature of Reason is that if we have access to the reality of things then we are God-like and have an intellectual and moral obligation to transcend this worldliness to achieve God-like greatness. The point behind the notion of Transcendentalism is to *go beyond* this worldliness to apprehension of ultimate reality and the way human beings ought to conduct themselves.

The Emersonian **"Over-Soul"** shares characteristics with Nietzsche's "Over-Man" or "Übermensch." For Nietzsche, human beings are entirely too willing to accept morality in which weakness and humility are considered "good." In *On the Genealogy of Morals*, Nietzsche made the famous distinction between master and slave moralities. The distinction is important for Nietzsche in making the case that early in human societies, people considered strength and power good and avoided weakness (considering it "bad") because weakness is conducive neither to the maintenance of life nor to the dignity and greatness of humanity. Perhaps an example to illustrate Nietzsche's conception of **master morality** will be sufficient to clarify the distinction.

Alexander the Great is said to have prayed to the gods prior to engaging in battle. But when he prayed, he did not ask the gods for assistance. He instead told them that he, like them, was great and powerful. He promised he would defeat his adversaries. Alexander was, in short, a Nietzschean Over-Man and an example of the Emersonian Over-Soul.

The Übermensch takes power and uses it to assert the fact that he is alive and that he intends to extend and expand his power. The Übermensch does this by defeating a worthy opponent or problem. To conquer an advancing army or to solve a human problem are expressions of power.

Against the Over-Man/Übermensch for Nietzsche is the "lamb" of **slave morality**. Slave morality comes about as a result of feelings of resentment among the weak directed at the powerful because they are powerful and a threat to those who are weak. Out of resentment of the powerful comes the contention of the weak that weakness is actually good while power is evil. For Nietzsche, this is a **transvaluation of values**. Meekness (or weakness) and humility are Christian virtues. Nietzsche (and Emerson) had little patience for the moral system that Christianity creates and sustains.

The "Divinity School Address" (1838), presented to the graduating class at Harvard University, contains Emerson's view of what religious doctrines *are* and what they *ought to* be. Emerson's position on religious thought is largely a reaction to forms of Christianity that separate the individual from God in thinking that humans constantly fail to live up to God's expectations. Emerson challenges traditional understanding of the relationship of the human being to God. "The American Scholar" (1837) and "Divinity School Address" contain much of what is required to understand the nature and value of religion and how a religious attitude ought to manifest itself. Emerson argued, for example, that prayers berate humanity. Preachers and religious activities ought instead to be uplifting and help people to understand and appreciate their value and power instead of dwelling constantly on sin and the separation of humankind from God.

Like other elements of Emerson's work, individualism is characteristic of his views on religion. Individuals are not to be swallowed up in the crowd and expected to fall into lockstep with it. Christianity is too formal and authoritative. It requires that we sit still, listen to someone else read from a book, and stand or kneel in unison while speaking the same prayers and engaging in the same rituals. Instead of the stultifying formality of organized, traditional religion, Emerson proposes that we should not receive *instruction* from another, but that we should receive *provocation*. What another person says is to be accepted or rejected by virtue of one's own mind, not accepted or rejected because someone else said it.

The individual being part of God means the individual is at the center of the universe. We are therefore made for greatness. To achieve greatness, we must be free of the chains of the past, tradition, and authority to allow creativity and authenticity to manifest themselves. An individual exhibits divine nature by having the courage to speak one's own mind and be one's own person.

The Emersonian human being will not remain content in living up to (perhaps the better description is that the Transcendentalist will not live down to) the expectations of society. The individual must live up to his own expectations as part of God. In social contexts, however, we often find ourselves conforming to the expectations of others. In conformity, humans become tools used to reach goals instead of being ends in ourselves.

Emerson maintains that society turns us into things rather than recognizing and maintaining us as human beings – as Man. We think of ourselves as what we do for a living instead of thinking of ourselves as human beings. So the farmer may be John Smith, but he identifies himself as "John Smith, the farmer" in which case he is more a farmer than a human being.

The scholar, instead of being "Man thinking" becomes one who thinks and reiterates what others have thought before him. The scholar ought to recognize that books written in the past have value to give inspiration, not to tell us what to do and what to think. Too many people satisfy themselves with mediocre existences dictated by the supposed wisdom of the past and what is written in books. But we should not allow books to become tyrants. When a person allows books, the past, and the opinions of others to guide him – or worse, to restrain him – in his thinking, he disparages his own thoughts simply because they are his own. What then happens is that at another time some other person will say exactly what one has already thought and one will shamefully take the opinion that was his own from someone else. Emerson's warning is that we protect ourselves from potential embarrassment at our own peril and to no useful end. We may end up embarrassed or shamed in either case, whether we speak the new idea or remain silent.

The solution to misplaced humility with respect to ideas and aspirations is that we must be nonconformists. In conformity, we deny the sacredness of our own minds. The conformist gives his autonomy to the crowd and to the expectations of others, thereby forgetting himself. We fear that society will tell us that we are inconsistent or trouble-makers when we think differently from others or when we think today something different from what we thought yesterday. The point for Emerson, however, is that today is different from yesterday and it is conceivable that yesterday's thoughts do not properly fit the conditions of today.

Self-reliant people trust themselves. Self-reliant scholars have a duty like that of the preacher – not to bemoan human existence as sinful and sordid but to provide hortatory teaching making us see that we are not chained to the past and to European ways of thinking. As self-reliant, we will develop a truly and uniquely American human being and an American society worthy of the human beings inhabiting it. We have an obligation to overcome obstacles keeping us from self-trust and preventing us from forging a society worthy of the self-reliant American.

Emerson's views on the nature of self-trust and property echo in some sense the Marxist concern that the world of things is valued over humanity, leading to **alienation**. For the Marxist, people in capitalist societies are stripped of humanity when the world of work becomes a means to an end rather than an end in itself. Marx said alienation takes several forms. One of them is alienation of man from his labor. Because we sell our labor to an employer (the capitalist), our labor no longer belongs to us. Since labor produces the product, the product, too, fails to belong to the person who creates it. This is the alienation of the human being from the product of labor and alienation of the person from himself. In addition, we become alienated from each other because we confront each other not as human beings but as workers who compete with each other for scarce employment.

Emerson's position on the moral life described in "Self-Reliance" and "The American Scholar" also anticipates the work of Nietzsche such that when we do not recognize power and nobility in ourselves (Emersonian pride and confidence in human greatness), we fall into pathetic existences accepting slave morality rather than gaining mastery over ourselves and society's expectations. That we have the capacity to create ourselves and challenge banal expectations is hateful to absolutists. That the "soul becomes" is contrary to foundations, static existence, conformity, and mediocrity – all of which are the stuff of rigid social expectations and oppressive governments.

Thoreau is in a sense a follower of Emerson, or at least he is a follower in the minimal sense in which a Transcendentalist can "follow" the lead of another person. Thoreau put into practice what Emerson told us we ought to do by intentionally "removing" himself from society and building a small cabin by Walden Pond where he wished to live quietly, in solitude, and deliberately.

In *Walden,* Thoreau takes great care to chronicle details of his two-year life in the woods and comments on the value of living simply. Emerson told us what Transcendentalism *is* while Thoreau showed us what it *can be.*

Emerson argued that the state is not superior to the citizens. The state is only an alterable expediency because we have the capacity to create a better state. Believing that we have the capacity and the right to alter or re-make the state echoes the sentiment of Thomas Jefferson who commented that rebellion is often a good thing. The same sentiment finds a home in Thoreau's work and life, especially since he argued for civil disobedience. The Transcendentalists, with their individualist attitude toward government, are in the good company of Paine who said governments exist as a necessary evil to soften our "wickedness." For Paine, it was unwise to trust that all other people will follow the dictates of morality and live together in peaceful and productive relations. Emerson seemed to find the nature of social existence much the same when he lamented in "Politics" that we live in a diminished condition when we pay tribute to governments created by force. Emerson the libertarian and near-anarchist contended that we are best off with less government with fewer laws and power. The way to solve the problem of abuse of government power is the development of private character to make government obsolete. While we are not living as autonomous beings with dignity and integrity, we need the state. Emerson makes the case plainly and simply by noting that the government we currently have is not the best one in existence, it is simply the best *for us* in this time given our condition. That it is the best for our condition does not mean that it is a good state since every state is corrupt when its people are corrupt.

Government will not effect needed change. If we want the state to change, we need to change it ourselves. Emerson *told* us how to change ourselves by reaching for transcendence of this world to the divine. Thoreau *showed* us how to connect with the divine in ourselves by living a (relatively) solitary and deliberate life near Walden Pond. He did it by practicing what both he and Emerson preached in not paying taxes to a corrupt government.

The state is therefore not our highest achievement. Needing a government shows individual growth to be incomplete, expressing the level of cultivation of its people. The individual of self-trust rejects government laws and procedures that limit thought and action to create conformity and complacency. Thoreau rejected all that by living in the woods and away from society to live simply, deliberately, and authentically. To live simply is to live without artificial desires and wants and to avoid the noise and confusion of a society growing by leaps and bounds, failing to see the forest because it has *cut down* the trees. If one lives outside the grasp of the state, one does not pay taxes. If one does not pay taxes, one is not forced to support institutions like slavery and the Mexican–American War, both of which Thoreau found morally repugnant. Living simply removes the need to protect things and to create governments to limit actions and thoughts, and then tax us for the privilege of doing so. It is possible in the woods to become and to be oneself and to march, as he put it, to the beat of a different drummer. Perhaps it is in the woods that one can learn that even when he returns to society, he can continue to express authentic being. There is no one to call you "weird" when you are alone; there is no one to force you to conform to "normalcy" when you are living by your own lights. When a person can learn to be alone in society and appreciates and lives according to his individuality, that is when the state can expire.

THE CONTINUING SPIRIT OF REFORM

W. E. B. DU BOIS

W. E. B. Du Bois (1868–1963) is well known for his study "**The Negro Problem**" and trying to find a solution to it. Du Bois was born in Massachusetts after the Civil War and did not experience first-hand the injustice of slavery. He was, however, well aware of persistent and pernicious problems of racial prejudice and tensions permeating American society. The work and arguments he produced are philosophically significant and an early expression of African American philosophy. African American philosophy arises from lived experience of slavery, oppression, discrimination, and denial of rights. It is at the same time a philosophy of strength and hope.

Two primary traditions in African American philosophy are **assimilationism** and **separatism**. For an assimilationist such as

Booker T. Washington, African Americans ought to try to gain acceptance of white Americans by achieving economic success. For a separatist, it is neither possible nor desirable for assimilation to occur. Du Bois held a mild form of separatism as a means to try to achieve social justice for African Americans.

Washington's assimilationist suggestions were that African Americans should cease agitating for change and access to higher education and instead concentrate on gaining skills to achieve economic success. With economic success, he claimed, they would then become respected by white Americans. Du Bois considered Washington's position unacceptable, countering that African American contributions in all realms, including education, would lead to acceptance in American society.

For Du Bois, "The Negro Problem" would be solved in two ways. First, the solution to immorality, crime, and laziness among African Americans, all arising from the heritage of slavery, would come from within the African American community. The second step would come from white Americans in being impartial in selecting people for inclusion in economic and intellectual worlds and fostering respect for people and their liberty regardless of race. Much to his dismay, white Americans usually did not do their part.

Du Bois argued for the **"Talented Tenth"** to be the starting point for racial equality and acceptance, and that **"double consciousness"** and the **"The Color Line"** were problems that must be solved to achieve African American solidarity, preserve African American culture, and overcome prejudice and injustice. Du Bois was not convinced that Booker T. Washington's proposals for African American advancement were wise or practical, and he was certain they were not consistent with self-respect. To acquiesce in racism and segregation, accepting a lesser position for African Americans as laborers and small business owners would deny the abilities and inherent dignity of African Americans.

Unlike Washington, who put the blame for African American poverty, crime, and social ills on African Americans, Du Bois, in his early work on blacks in Philadelphia, concluded from careful empirical study that the social condition of African Americans stemmed directly from the institution of slavery and continuing racist tendencies among whites to keep African Americans in low social positions. Du Bois would not leave it to white Americans to solve the problems of black Americans. Race solidarity is instead the solution to "The Negro Problem" in African Americans finding refuge in their own community, believing in their own destiny, and trusting in their own ability and worth.

It is not only in the civic realm that "The Negro Problem" and its solution manifest themselves. Du Bois realized the very significant impact of religious belief on African Americans. While not personally "religious," Du Bois promoted the notion central to **Black Liberation Theology** that the plight of African Americans is like that of Jesus. Jesus was a laborer, poor, despised, persecuted, and killed – and so are African Americans.

Du Bois did not hesitate to point out that spineless assimilationism of Washington's kind was a contributing factor in denial of African American rights, creation of "**Jim Crow" laws**, and lack of support for African American education. What mattered, for Du Bois, was whether African Americans were able to rise from abject conditions through pride in themselves and their heritage.

Du Bois proposed that the "Talented Tenth" of African Americans should attain levels of higher education and social action to serve as proof of the worth and ability of African Americans. Washington's proposal was certainly not working, especially given what Du Bois saw through a Marxist social stance as another aspect of "The Negro Problem." All the characteristics of **capitalism** plague all workers, but African Americans suffer the problems of capitalism even more acutely than other workers because African Americans are not only exploited by capitalists, they are also persecuted by the prejudice of white workers.

"The Negro Problem," overall, is caused and exacerbated in two ways. One is "The Color Line" that seems to know no boundaries, being as much in the church as in secular society. African Americans usually founded their own churches, finding themselves unwelcome in ones dominated by whites.

"The Negro Problem" is also compounded by "Double Consciousness," which Du Bois described early in *The Souls of Black Folk* (1903) as a condition in which the world allows him no true self-consciousness because he feels himself as "twoness," in being an American and an African, where he has two souls and his strivings are recognized in neither of them. The point is that the African American wishes to be both African and American, but to be so without being persecuted by others. Double consciousness justifies both African American solidarity and separatism. Du Bois argued that African Americans wish to be part of American culture and to use their talents and powers that have been wasted in the past. They should be wasted no more.

EMMA GOLDMAN

Emma Goldman, a Russian immigrant, came to the U.S. in 1885 hoping to live and experience the "American Dream." What she found were injustices and inequalities affecting men and women alike and social structures and expectations that exacerbated problems of oppression, inequality, and injustice. Goldman was a prolific writer, agitator, and activist. The focus in this chapter is on her work on Marxist anarchism and the problems of patriotism and woman suffrage.

The Marxists' goal is to do away with the state all together. It will wither away from cooperation among free people conceiving of their relationships such that everyone will work and contribute to society according to their abilities, and everyone will receive from society what they need to live a good life. In capitalist society, however, people are paid wages that are not commensurate with the value of things produced. Capitalists, owners of the means of production, provide the lowest possible wage to the workers that is consistent with their mere survival.

The capitalist can survive longer than the workers as a result of the increasing value of the world of "things" produced by workers such that the capitalist, who pays for labor, keeps the products of labor and sells or trades them for more than the price paid to the worker for producing them. Profits are then in the hands of the capitalist who has control of **surplus value**. The surplus value is capital, or "stored labor." As Marx described it, profit received allows the capitalist more security than the worker. In addition, a minimal living wage paid to workers who compete with each other for scarce employment makes workers competitors with each other and this further decreases the value of labor. The less labor is valued and paid, the more profit the capitalist can accumulate. Work becomes, for the workers, simply a means of subsistence.

Even worse is that in a capitalist society the thing produced from labor becomes alien to the worker so that the more he works, the less he is valued. Marx's view was that this is much like what happens with a religion such that the more a person puts into God, the less he has of himself. In a capitalist system, labor is external to the worker rather than part of his humanity. Labor simply satisfies other needs and is not a deep need in itself. The laborer sells his labor and effectively sells himself. The upshot of capitalism, then, is that the human being is alienated from his labor, from himself, from the product he makes, and ultimately from other human beings.

Communism is "the **negation of the negation.**" The human being is no longer alienated from himself, from his labor and its products, or from other people. In this idyllic condition, work is release and production of human energy rather than merely a means of base subsistence. Emma Goldman adopted this ethical Marxist stance and expressed it in adherence to anarchism. Contrary to commonly held beliefs, anarchism is not a free-for-all with a Hobbesian war of all against all. In "Anarchism: What it Really Stands For," anarchism is not restricted by artificial laws created by a government resting on violence. Anarchism teaches unity between individuals and their social being. Governments, on the other hand, pit people against each other and require subordination of human beings to man-made laws, principles, and strained social organization. While capitalism forces people to work for mere subsistence, anarchism allows for the creation of perfect personalities who will work because it is inspiring, the satisfaction of a deep human need. Goldman argued that anarchism liberates people from religion, from property, and from government. In a manner reminiscent of Thoreau's civil disobedience, Goldman's anarchism is defiance and resistance to laws and restrictions of all kinds. Anarchism centers on individual sovereignty and social harmony. It has clear affinities to Thoreau and Emerson in celebrating the individual, and to Stanton on the need for self-sovereignty.

Since Goldman argued for no political state, it is no surprise that she found patriotism morally questionable. In "Patriotism: A Menace to Liberty" (1917) Goldman described patriotism as a self-respect- and dignity-reducing superstition that increases arrogance. Patriotism divides the world into "little spots" surrounded by gates. If you are born in some particular spot, you are "better" than someone else who was born in a different spot. The result is violence in discharging a duty to fight others to prove superiority. So while the non-anarchist believes that anarchism is chaos and violence, Goldman shows that it is militarism and patriotism that are violent and far from moral.

In "Woman **Suffrage**" (1910), Goldman argues *against* women's right to vote. It may seem odd at first, especially given that her convictions indicated firm belief in the equal dignity and rights of men and women, that she would argue against woman suffrage. It is, however, perfectly consistent with her views on the evils of patriotism and government systems.

The exercise of the right to vote is just as much a form of oppression and violence as government. To have the right to vote is nothing more than the right to coerce others to obey the rules of the majority. To think that women will in some way make government and its processes better by voting is, for Goldman, irrational. Women have no special power to improve government. They are simply human beings.

When the oppressed have the right to vote, they are not made better by it. Instead, what improves human beings, and especially a woman, is to assert her personality, to deny anyone else the right to her body, to refuse to have children unless she wants them, and not to be a servant of anyone, whether the "master" is God, government, society, a husband or family, or anyone else.

CRITICISMS

For all the Transcendentalists' claims to uniqueness and revolutionary thinking, and for all the inspiration their words create, Transcendentalism could not maintain a hold on American action. That it continues to capture the imaginations of Americans and people around the world is indisputable. The New England Transcendentalists spoke a language understandable by Americans who recognize and remember their revolutionary heritage. There is always room for improvement, change happens whether we like it or not, and the point of it all is to make the best world we are capable of building. With all their exhortations to courage and self-reliance, to individualism and the power of the human spirit, there is still something missing in New England Transcendentalism. Emerson and Thoreau both insisted that their work was practical, but what is missing is real application of the ideals they propounded.

The America existing after the American Revolution and well past the Civil War saw revolutionary action play itself out in the creation of bustling metropolises, railroad lines that allowed (relatively) speedy and reliable travel, and a growing system of commerce and capitalist activity never before seen in America. America is a nation of action and nearly unbounded energy. What the Transcendentalists seemed to put forth is something decidedly different. Thoreau represented in *Walden* was not a man of unbounded energy who sought to build railroads, run factories, or engage in business. Emerson was unlikely to have worked in manufacturing. Emerson and Thoreau tell us that we have a duty to shrink government and expand human dignity by recognizing and acting on a divine spark in ourselves – but this really tells us nothing about what we ought to do to get by in the world. Saying the state will expire when individuals are wise does not provide any helpful guide to know what to do except in the whimsical sense in which Emerson and Thoreau state their cases.

Thoreau would certainly disagree with the notion that Transcendentalism fails to tell us what to do in the world since he went into the woods with the explicit purpose to show how it was to be done. But what practical-minded American would take Thoreau's approach seriously or for any considerable period of time? Certainly, Americans go camping and out "roughing it," but we tend to do that on weekends, for fun, not to "find ourselves" or to "live deliberately." We do it to get away from the rat race, to get away from cities, to get away from other people.

Getting away from other people is part of the problem with Transcendentalism. The Transcendentalist basically tells us to throw traditions and authority away, but can we truly do this in the way in which Emerson and Thoreau said it could be done? Living in the woods is well and good for people who are healthy and strong enough to build their own cabins and grow their own food, but not all of us are capable of doing so. The simple fact is that we need division of labor among human beings so that our lives are made less, not more, unpleasant. To live as a Transcendentalist, truly to take it seriously, would be to evade problems rather than to try to solve them. Going out into the woods to avoid paying taxes, or refusing to pay them in opposition to war and slavery, does very little actually to slow or stop the escalation of war or to end slavery.

Perhaps if all people stopped paying their taxes, there would be no way to support a war or to catch fugitive slaves. But people do not all wish to retreat into the woods to find authentic being.

For the Transcendentalist, to be an authentic human being is to live according to one's own lights. But what if living by my lights is different from how you live by yours?

How can we decide, on the Transcendentalist's view of the nature of knowledge, which of two competing claims is false when the way in which we determine what is true is by the feeling that we are right? The Transcendentalist's position on the nature of knowledge and reality approximates the metaphysics and epistemology of Immanuel Kant but it never comes close enough to convince us that there is anything more to Transcendentalism than a sincere conviction that we can, through experience in the world, come to truths outside of it. The Transcendentalist's philosophy of religion flies in the face of traditional Christian doctrine and is unlikely to be accepted and acted upon by the majority of American Christians.

The condition of Transcendentalist thinking might be much like that of the **Stoic**s. The Stoics were convinced that we ought to approach the world and its problems with an even mind, that we should not allow ourselves to be flustered by things we cannot change. The irony here is that this is, as someone once said, a great philosophy until you really need one. While the ethics and social thought of the New England Transcendentalists is inspiring, we may justifiably ask how we can expect all human beings to develop the wisdom of the Transcendentalist and need no government. The Transcendentalist contends that because we provide the moral law to ourselves and recognition of it is identical to the recognition of it by all others, we should be able, in principle, to act on such wisdom. It is, however, unfortunately beyond doubt that there are people who will never reach the level of individual or social maturity and wisdom required of Transcendentalism, and for that reason alone, the expiration of the state or even an extremely minimalist conception of political organization is unlikely to find practical use and value.

On the other hand, the thought of the New England Transcendentalists found some expression and use in the Abolitionist movement we saw in Chapter 4 and in the work of Stanton on self-sovereignty. Self sovereignty, like self-reliance, is both the means to and the goal of a human life of authenticity and integrity.

Du Bois' position on the "Talented Tenth" may be a form of elitism indicating that only the truly exceptional human being has the capacity to make significant and long-lasting contributions to the progress of African Americans. It also underestimates the percentage of African Americans who have the capacity to make such contributions. Further, Du Bois, like most men of his time, largely ignored the plight of African American women in writing and speaking on the concerns of men.

Goldman's Marxist anarchism is idealistic and hopeful, but probably not practical. To argue for a society of free, autonomous agents living a life unfettered by the chains of government discounts what many may take to be a fact of human life: that we are competitive individuals encumbered by communities whose lives are often centrally defined by them. Goldman's idealistic anarchism may be too individualistic in failing to recognize the possibility that people are not all creative beings striving to realize their potential simply because the potential is there. Goldman's characterization of patriotism is exaggerated and arguably an unfair description of the meaning of "home" that happens to be a political one for the patriot. It is not always that the patriotic American thinks all others are of less value because they happen not to have been born in this "spot." Patriotism can take other forms, including pride in one's own contributions and achievements within a particular geopolitical region.

It is possible that the anarchist's way of life is one to which practitioners develop a pernicious attachment and from which they will oppress others and stifle their creativity. This is one of the complaints that many capitalists lodge against collectivist Marxists – that creativity and freedom are restricted when subjected to the expectation that people will abandon capitalistic competitive conditions for the idyllic conditions Goldman has described.

While Goldman's assessment of the immorality of woman suffrage – and indeed of all political activity – has some force, it was perhaps remiss of her to argue against the elective franchise for women who were and are part of a political society in which the right to vote is not always used to restrict the rights of others, but is often part of the enlargement of rights instead. In this, Goldman's position may be exaggerated and extreme, ignoring the good that political participation may do while people are subjects of governments.

CONCLUSION

The New England Transcendentalists, along with Du Bois and Goldman, are representative of the kinds of activism for change and social justice that characterized much of American thought. American Pragmatism takes up where Transcendentalism left off, and movements in Native American and African American philosophy, the rise of American feminist theory, and continued theorizing about the clash between the individual and the community continue in American society.

FURTHER READING

For the New England Transcendentalists, see Edward H. Madden, *Civil Disobedience and Moral Law in Nineteenth Century American Philosophy* (Seattle: University of Washington Press, 1968); Stephen Hahn, *On Thoreau* (Belmont, CA: Wadsworth, 2000); and Robert D. Richardson, *Emerson: The Mind on Fire* (Berkeley: University of California Press, 1995). There are many web sites on which the work of the Transcendentalists may be found in their entirety.

For Goldman, see especially her own essays in *Anarchism and Other Essays* (Port Washington, NY: Kennikat Press, 1969), available free online in *The Emma Goldman Papers* at http://sunsite.berkeley.edu/goldman/. A short and accessible biography is Leslie A. Howe's *On Goldman* (Belmont, CA: Wadsworth, 2000). See also John Chalberg, *Emma Goldman: American Individualist* (New York: Harper Collins, 1991). On Du Bois, see especially Brian Johnson, ed., *Du Bois on Reform* (Lanham: Alta Mira, 2005); Phil Zuckerman, ed., *Du Bois on Religion* (Walnut Creek: Alta Mira, 2000); and Juguo Zhang, *The Quest for the Abolition of the Color Line* (New York: Routledge, 2001).

6

THE PRAGMATISTS

THE NATURE OF PRAGMATISM

Fundamentally important for American philosophers is determining what philosophy is and what the philosopher is to do. Many American philosophers insist on the practical value of speculative inquiry. We saw this in the work of Franklin in his quest to understand ethics for practice. We saw it in revolutionaries like Paine and Goldman who did not spin fanciful theories or abstract principles simply to know something about freedom, rights, and justice, but to *do* something about them.

American Pragmatists elaborate on change and method to determine philosophy's purpose. For other American philosophers whose goal is action for change, the pragmatists provide the meaning and workings of philosophical method arising from change and using change to make a difference. Recognizing the inevitability of change, Pragmatists reject notions of fixity, finality, and certainty, adopting an attitude of fallibilism regarding all scientific, metaphysical, epistemological, moral, and social claims. The Pragmatist rejects absolute truth and teleology, instead holding that what is expedient or what "works" is true because it makes a difference in living our lives. The Pragmatist is satisfied with the notion that "truth" becomes and changes just like all other things in this world, and truth and change are indifferent to the needs, desires, and interests of people.

Even though American Pragmatists reject **teleology**, there is a general tendency among much of the American population in actual "practice" to look toward final ends and goals, to have a conception of **human nature** (of the way people "really are") and to think of knowledge as something "out there" to be perceived and held as information for its own sake. While the Pragmatist does not deny that knowledge is important, we must understand the value of knowledge in making a concrete difference in our lives.

There were and are many American Pragmatists, but here I concentrate primarily on four of the most prominent American Pragmatists to provide an overview of what Pragmatism is, what it means and what it implies. They are Charles Sanders Peirce (1839–1914), William James (1842–1910), John Dewey (1859–1952), and Richard Rorty (1931–2007). To understand the genesis of American Pragmatism, we will also look to the work of Chauncey Wright (1830–75), an ardent supporter of Charles Darwin's (1809–82) theory of evolution from *On the Origin of Species* (1859) as a springboard for understanding the place of evolutionary thinking in the development of American Pragmatism.

Pragmatism is not so much a fully worked out theory as a method of doing philosophy. For the pragmatist, the point is to change the world, not simply to try in some analytical and abstract fashion to understand it. The Pragmatists reject all a priori claims and abstract speculation not because they fail to find such things interesting, but because they find a way in which interest in them moves philosophy from the purely speculative to the practical. Pragmatists avoid building full-fledged theories of the nature of reality, knowledge, or the good life because they realize that facts and theories are properly combined with experience, all of which are changeable. Dewey thought of his work as a **"reconstruction" in philosophy** to advance public well-being. In this way, his work is idealistic and speculative, but it is first and foremost practical.

Pragmatism may also be considered – as Dewey certainly did consider it – as a solution to problems that plague modern society. Dewey noted that there is a lack of consistency between what we say we will do to solve our problems using traditional philosophy and what we actually do. What we in fact do to solve our problems is to look immediately to empirical means in the natural world. What we often say about empirical means and the natural world are completely different things. We often say that things of ordinary, everyday lived experience are unworthy of the finality of perfect theory. The long and the short of it can be expressed in an example. **Creationists** hold a doctrine of fixity and finality in the natural world, including the notion that everything was created at once, by God, to be exactly as it is and that species never change or mutate. Creationists on the whole, however, do not hesitate in actual experience to take a new antibiotic to treat an infection when the old antibiotic ceases to be effective. Evolution indicates that the bacterial infection has grown immune to the antibiotic and as a result it is necessary to switch to a different one to kill the infection. It is ironic how people, as Dewey noted, live a dual existence between what they do and what they think. In other words, the absolutist lives a life of contradiction.

CHAUNCEY WRIGHT AND EVOLUTION

The history of human thought includes countless references to the natural development of purposes in the universe. Some examples we have already seen are found in the works of Paine, Jefferson, and Franklin. Going back much farther, Aristotle argued for purpose in nature, that there are natural kinds, and that things are fit for specific purposes. Such views of design and purpose may seem innocent and simple enough – and they are even now very popularly held beliefs. Paine, Franklin, Jefferson, and Edwards all thought that there is purpose in the world given from "on high." But is it really this simple and is it really so innocent after all?

The **Argument from Design** is alive with errors in reasoning and questionable claims. It is based on a bad analogy for the simple fact that there is no other world in our experience to which we might appropriately compare this one. To be of good quality, analogical arguments require that reasonably similar things be compared. The Argument from Design commits the "**Birthday Fallacy**" in the assumption that since everything must have *a cause* that everything must have the *same cause*, and perhaps worst of all for those who employ it to try to prove that God exists, it makes no claims at all regarding a god of worship, kindness, or knowledge. Moreover, some who occupied themselves with design and purpose, such as Aristotle, reached conclusions we now recognize as more than simply questionable. Among them are that there are "natural kinds" and fixed species. From this way of thinking, Aristotle concluded that men are superior to women, that the male form is the ultimate, primary, and perfect form of humanity and that being female is an "accident" of gestation or a mistake of nature. Add to this that belief in design often leads to absolutism, **totalitarianism**, and **racism**, and we have a belief system that provides for odd and clearly unacceptable actions in moral and social contexts, not to mention peculiar mystical and metaphysical **ad hoc** explanations of occurrences in the natural world.

Alternately, the benefits of scientific thought are its usefulness and productivity. Science, in short, helps us to build and create. Explanations based on science do not and should not lend themselves to mysticism and ignorance, to totalitarianism and cruelty. Science should be used to enhance the ability to explain and live in the world.

Those who doubt that science is superior to religious or mystical explanations may believe also that science and religion can never peacefully co-exist. But for Chauncey Wright this is clearly not the case since, as he put it in "Natural Theology as a Positive Science" (1865), progress in science is the same as progress in religious truth. Knowledge frees us from errors arising through ignorance and superstition by exposing errors in both philosophy and religion. Wright was so confident of the value of science that he contended that if religious truth is refuted or changed by progress in knowledge, we ought to think that the teachings of such religions were actually superstitions, and not that science is irreligious. If there are evils arising from science, it is the fault of bad reasoning and inquiry among theologians and not the fault of science.

Darwin's theory of evolution is even in our time regularly attacked and its adherents cajoled for "irreligious" teachings, lack of faith, and stubborn inability or unwillingness to see design in the universe. Chauncey Wright, however, defended the theory of evolution while at the same time avoiding opposition to religious belief. He was able to hold firm to convictions in both realms because he held that religious claims are accepted on emotional grounds while those of science are accepted on rational grounds. By the process of rational scientific inquiry, we find that natural selection (evolution) has no goals or purposes of its own. Instead, evolution is a process without a mind. While there is change, change is simply a fact.

Further, Wright argues that there is nothing "special" about being human (contrary to those who believe that we were put here for some Godly purpose as part of an ultimate plan) and that our power of self-awareness is simply a different power, apparently, from that which other animals possess. It means that we are not the "top of the line" of Creation and there is nothing special or divine about us.

It is imperative for understanding the place of the theory of evolution in the world of Wright, and indeed in that of all the Pragmatists, to be clear on definitions of key terms. The theory of evolution is a scientific biological theory regarding the origin of species and the process of natural selection. It refers to the way in which biological organisms change or adapt to their environments and what constitutes fitness for species' continued survival in the environments in which they live. Because this is the case, the theory of evolution does not include reference to final, ultimate ends or to purposes, fixity, and finality in the universe.

A term related to the theory of evolution is "**positivism**." Positivism is a way of conceiving of method in science related to the meanings of moral, scientific, and other terminology. For the positivist, statements are meaningful when they are verifiable in fact or in principle. Meaningless statements tend to populate metaphysics, and while terms in metaphysics may have meaning within a metaphysical system, they are not scientific statements regarding facts. We cannot therefore test them, verify them, falsify them, or do anything with them except find them intellectually curious and interesting fictions.

Evolutionism is a kind of "extension" (warranted or not) of the Darwinian theory of evolution in which adherents claim that the biological theory applies to social processes. An evolutionist may believe, for example, that a capitalistic system of economic activity in which stronger capitalists "beat" their weaker opponents in the economic realm is the way things ought to be. Evolutionism has a moral tone to it that is not justified by the descriptive and explanatory function of the biological theory.

With clarified terms and concepts in hand, it is also important to note that the process of evolution depends on causes and effects on which empirical science on the whole depends. This does not mean that there are implications for the social world. Wright's conception of the use of the theory of evolution in science does not necessitate becoming a social Darwinist because evolution is not "progress." It is simply change.

PRAGMATIST EPISTEMOLOGY AND METAPHYSICS

Peirce's view of the nature of knowledge is, like the Pragmatists after him, that it is tentative at best. This does not mean there is no point in seeking knowledge. Knowledge and its very close relative, belief, are what drive us to action. Belief, Peirce claimed, goes hand in hand with a habit that leads to action. Doubt, however, does not produce action as habit but instead produces action to relieve annoyance caused by doubt. Peirce noted, for example, that if we look to the ways in which people really behave with respect to what they call "knowledge," we find that their desire to know comes about as a result of feeling uncomfortable because of the presence of doubt. When a person doubts some claim or wishes to solve a problem but does not at that moment know how to solve it, the search is on for a way to "fix," situate, or firmly establish the claim, statement, or process. "Fixing" it results in a feeling of satisfaction in being convinced that one has solved the problem or gained knowledge. The feeling of satisfaction is pleasant and since people rarely wish to move themselves from a pleasant and comfortable feeling to a feeling of distraction, disturbance, and discomfort, they call "knowledge" the satisfaction they feel in the claims they make or the processes in which they have engaged. Peirce, however, is not convinced that what we possess in those cases is knowledge. It is, instead, belief.

In "The Fixation of Belief" (1877), Peirce argued that there are four methods of fixing or establishing beliefs and none of the first three fits well with experience or actual human behavior. Because they do not fit with experience and behavior, they are unsuccessful methods. They are also out of touch with the social nature of knowledge. The **method of tenacity**, more fit for hermits than social human beings, is that a belief is formed and then held under such protective care that the person holding a belief in this way will go to great lengths to ensure that she will not endanger the belief by exposure to contrary or different opinions. It is inevitable that some stray thought will make its way into her mind or that some other person will disagree with what she thinks. If she attends to the other person's view or the possibility that she may be wrong in her own thoughts, she will fall again into the agitation of doubt. To combat agitation, she may find it useful to turn to the **method of authority**, an often particularly malicious means of fixing belief, in which a group of like-minded people combine strength and belief to ensure re-confirmation of what they already believe and ensure that no contrary opinions creep in to their comfortable position. This method of fixing belief is often malicious and cruel in that it is the method employed, for example, by Inquisitors who spared no method of punishing and torturing those who thought differently from them. We know that the method of authority used in the **Spanish Inquisition** ultimately failed, and it will fail, too, even when the method of authority is used "benignly" in accomplishing its goals (for example, by "social norming" or creating pressure to conform and eliciting shame or embarrassment in others for not complying with expectations). It is inevitable that a closed society cannot long isolate itself from outside influences, and just like the method of tenacity, people will find their "comfort zones" invaded, resulting in doubt replacing the comfort of belief.

The previously tenacious or authoritarian believer might seek refuge in a third method, the method of **a priori rationalism** which depends on the notion that "pure reason" dictates that what we believe is right, true, and good. While this method is on its face intellectually superior to the methods of tenacity and authority, it really is not so. We have numerous indications of the failure of this method since, for example, one person may believe that it is firmly within the bounds of reason to believe that there are innate ideas while another thinks it equally rational to believe there are no innate ideas at all. Who is right? The answer is that it is not possible to determine which of them is right and arguments between and among them end in failure since one will hold just as tightly to belief in innate ideas as the other will to experience as the origin of ideas. Their arguments fall by the wayside, ignored in favor of the comfort of established belief.

In place of failed methods of belief-fixing, Peirce offers the **method of science**. Where two of the three methods rely on individuals (tenacity and a priori rationalism) and the method of authority depends on group cohesion and power (or on what we might today call "group-think"), the method of science relies on experiment and verification. The benefit of experiment and verification is that the method of science is like experiences themselves. Experiences are variable and subject to change and so, too, are the conclusions of the method of science. Using the method of science, we are prepared to alter or abandon positions when they are no longer confirmed or verified by evidence. An added bonus of this method is benefit to be gained in free, open discussion and inquiry concerning the beliefs we hold so they may be modified or abandoned to increase effective action in the world. For example, where the a priori rationalist might affirm freedom of the will on the basis of a very strong feeling that it is right, and this feeling is considered an indication of the rationality of the belief, the Peirceian Pragmatist will affirm (or deny, or perhaps even throw the question away as unanswerable) the belief only if it passes certain tests of meaning and verification.

Peirce maintained in "The Fixation of Belief" that "Reals" exist by claiming that such things are independent of our opinions and they can be ascertained by reasoning. The method of science combines our predilection to alleviate doubt through a quest for knowledge and it takes into consideration that observation and experiment are required for verification of the reality of things and the meanings of the statements we make about them.

For Peirce in "How to Make Our Ideas Clear" (1878) the "**Pragmatic Maxim**" is to ask ourselves what kind of practical effect our ideas have. What we understand of effects is what the object is. Epistemology is central in Peirce's rejection of metaphysics and is evidenced in his view of the nature of meaning. A statement is meaningful when it can be put to a test. Suppose we are looking at two rings, both of which are said to have diamonds in them but there is no discernible difference between them. Putting them to further test to determine whether they contain genuine diamonds or imitations will tell us what we need to know. Prior to that, there is no difference between the two rings.

For Peirce, metaphysical claims about existence or the nature of reality cannot be verified. In "What Pragmatism Is" (1905) he argued that instead of saying that we want the truth, we should simply admit that what we want is belief that is safe from doubt. We cannot know the nature of "reality," but we can use the method of science to provide us with approximations about it. The best we can do is to formulate our beliefs with as much evidence and reliability as we can – and then move on from there.

James' epistemology and metaphysics are much like those of Peirce with respect to the effects of our knowledge (or belief) claims. James, however, adds clarity to the notion that Pragmatism is a method and that the function of philosophy is to determine what difference it will make if we think that some theory, belief or proposition is true (or not). It is not profitable or necessary to give our attention to – or even to try to derive – final formulations of "the way things are." For James, all conclusions and activities of science are approximations. The most important point is what we do with results of inquiries.

But what of truth? With respect to the question of truth it is important to recognize a unique contribution, James' **Pragmatic Theory of Truth**, a competitor of traditional correspondence and coherence theories.

The **correspondence theory of truth** is often considered "common sense." Its adherents claim there is a reality outside us composed of qualities perceived with the senses and mediated through ideas. The assumption is that our ideas more or less copy, or represent, things as they actually are. The long and the short of it is that it may just be too common and it may not, in fact, make much sense.

If we believe that ideas are copies or representations of things as they actually are, but "knowledge" of the external world is mediated through ideas (no one really thinks that his mind "becomes" a tree or "has" a tree in it when perceiving the tree), there is clearly a fundamental lack of connection between things as they are and our perceptions of them. We can never be sure that what we see (or perceive in any other way) is what actually exists outside our thoughts. We are not really sure that there is a world outside us at all. Berkeley took this problem so far as to argue that there are no material objects, that it is contradictory to think they exist, and that God would not bother to create them. William James was aware of all of these and many other problems with the correspondence theory of truth and the **causal theory of perception** and recognized that it simply will not do if what we seek is some meaningful statement of what is real and what we can know about it.

The **coherence theory of truth** might be worse than correspondence since it makes no reference whatsoever to a world beyond the act of thinking and reorganizing ideas in the mind. On the coherence theory, statements are true when they "cohere" in a system of ideas. For example, the Euclidean system of geometry makes sense within itself but there are competing geometries that are themselves self-consistent while being inconsistent with each other. For the coherence theorist, a theory is appropriate and the statements it generates are true when they are consistent with each other, generating no contradictions and absurdities. The problem with this view, though, is that it makes knowledge little more than reorganization of thoughts and taking care in spinning stories about reality and knowledge to ensure that no statement conflicts with any other. For any Pragmatist, using the coherence theory is certainly no way to go about getting things done or finding value in what we claim to know. James provides an alternative.

The Pragmatic Theory of Truth is essentially that truth is made, not discovered. The reason we seek truth (and knowledge) is to get things done, find value in what we do, and have a meaning in life. We seek knowledge for what we can do with it, whether it is to cure a disease or to get from one place to another. We do not seek health for the sake of health itself, but because it is beneficial for us to be healthy.

Truth is not in a theory or a statement. It is instead that truth "happens" to a theory or statement. Statements become true by the occurrence of events, by a process. James asked what practical difference an idea being true makes in anyone's life. To answer this question, we look for ideas we can use, corroborate, and verify in experience to find practical consequences. James relates an example about someone who is lost in a forest and happens upon a cow path. Prior to being lost in the woods, the claim that "there is a cow path in the forest" was true, but it made no difference to anyone who had no need to know it was there. When someone is lost, however, things change. The cow path indicates to the wayward traveler that there is probably a farm nearby, and to find the farm is to find other people, and to find other people is to find out one's location, and hence not to be lost. It is all very practical. The Pragmatist does not claim there was never any cow path in the woods until the lost traveler saw it. It is simply the case that it made no concrete difference in anyone's life (other than, perhaps, to cows) that the path was there. Once the perception of the cow path has been processed and used, the claim "There is a cow path in the forest" has practical value and meaning – and it is true. It is simply useful information. The existence and knowledge of the existence of the cow path amounts to practical consequences that have "cash value," i.e., they are practical. This is reality. Reality is what truths have to account for. What we have to account for are sensations, the ideas we have, and previous truths (such as that cow paths are known to lead to farms or to some useful place) we already know. There is no more reason to amuse ourselves with questions about whether "There is a cow path in the forest" is true right now or for all eternity. It will help no one to solve the problem of being lost by noting that the cow path has always been there and that it is true that this is so. James saw that the important thing in knowledge acquisition and knowledge claims is consequences. To insist on absolute knowledge is a weakness. We need adequate reasons for actions and explanations of things to solve problems. What we need, for James, is what he is supplying: a method of philosophical inquiry telling us that theories are not ends in themselves. They are useful pieces of information when and if they are successful in helping to solve problems.

In "What Pragmatism Means" (1907) James argued that we are to settle metaphysical disputes by the practical consequences holding them to be true will create. The example of the difference between Locke and Berkeley on the existence of matter is sufficient to clarify the point. Berkeley himself admitted, perhaps inadvertently, that the whole issue is one of verbal distinctions. When Berkeley noted in *The Principles of Human Knowledge* (1710) that "philosophers raise a dust and then complain that they cannot see," he admitted that a simpler solution to problems is much better, preferable, and more efficient than complicated theories that are intellectually curious but useless. Berkeley admitted that sciences will proceed just as they have and as they will whether we are **materialists** or idealists. Holding to one position or the other, practically speaking, makes no difference. So for the very practical Pragmatist, what is the point in trying to determine whether the materialist or the idealist is right? If the consequences of their positions in science and matters of truth are no different from each other, then it is not productive to spend time and energy trying to figure out which one of them has a handle on the nature of reality. This does not mean that such disputes are necessarily useless in every instance. But if there is an instance in which metaphysical disputes are useless, then the differences are distinctions without differences, and we are better off channeling our energies and inquiries in another direction. In this view, it is the Pragmatist who is a much more rational defender of reason than the philosophers who stay in the Berkeleyan dust.

It is difficult to know exactly where to begin with Dewey since his interests and voluminous writings span many topics and many years. Dewey, like the other Pragmatists, maintained that a world of fixity and finality was not worthy of our intellectual, social, or moral attention. Dewey goes farther than the other Pragmatists, however, in making much more of the moral and social nature of this fact of Pragmatism. Dewey's view is that the history of philosophy is filled with theories about the origin, value, and character of knowledge, but all theories denying change are misdirected and mistaken. Because Dewey's philosophy is influenced significantly by Darwin's theory of evolution, he saw that we, like all other natural living things, are biological beings subject to change or mutation. Our environment changes, and we must change right along with it.

The effects of Darwin's theory are simple. The theory of evolution makes us realize that we should change traditional ways of thinking about the nature of philosophy and turn away from absolutism. Turning away from absolutism, for Dewey, means that real intellectual progress takes place when we abandon questions from traditional philosophy. Pragmatism makes us realize that we do not solve traditional philosophical problems at all. We simply get over them – and move on. The world in which we live presents problems to be overcome and we respond to them more or less intelligently. The more intelligent responses allow us to get by in the world. For as long as responses to problems help us to deal with them, we continue to act on responses as **habits** of behavior. We embrace habits not as absolute truths to be revered, but instead as methods or instruments to be used to continue solving problems – at least until we meet problems we are not able to solve. It is then that our senses and reactions come into full swing, leading to new possibilities to try to solve emergent problems. If and when our attempts at solutions are successful, they become new habits of action.

Absolutists, traditional rationalists, and empiricists failed to see that we are active in the production of knowledge and not passive spectators. Dewey's theory takes active knowledge into account. We are builders and doers who experience the world and try to solve problems. Traditional philosophers, however, looked to fixity and finality. Their view leads to the notion that change is to be avoided, that it is inconsistent with intelligence, and that it is an affront to perfection.

For the worlds of the ancient and medieval philosophers who lacked the scientific acumen possessed in the modern world, it made sense to them to fall back on the notion that there is purpose and design in the world making things the way they are and that, in addition, they give us reason to worship and pray to the creator of purpose and design. The theory of evolution, however, questions teleological doctrines and puts a crimp in belief in design.

Scientists and philosophers who wished to retain teleology as well as to embrace evolution often tried to arrange arguments to have it both ways. They did this primarily by maintaining that God designed things so that an ultimate design occurs over time through changes that are part of the design. It is easy enough to defeat this claim by noting that if variations cause adaptations leading more effectively to the survival of a species, adding the proposition that there is an intelligent plan in all of it is an ad hoc postulation of no value in knowing or explaining anything.

People who resort to absolutes, finality, and purposiveness do so because they have not come to grips with the fact that the world is composed of problems, some of which are completely intractable, and that we often create even more problems in retreating to the old style philosophy that gave us problems like appearance versus reality, the problem of evil, and others. In short, people seek certainty because they distrust themselves. In this, Dewey takes the Emersonian exhortation to "Trust Thyself" to systematic philosophical heights. The philosophical problems we have not solved because we cannot solve them are simply things we ought, in Dewey's view, to "get over." We ought to give up the quest for certainty because all we know is tentative, subject to revision, and, in a word, contingent. Thinking there is absolute truth leads us to believe we are not participants in knowledge, but when we recognize that there is no absolute truth it gives us the freedom to give credit to new ideas that we can subject to further tests and to correct or abandon them by experience.

What remains now is how to solve problems in ethics and social life by using the Deweyan conception of Pragmatism. That our knowledge is tentative and changeable is applicable to the sciences as well as to our moral and social lives. The ideas we form and employ are tools or instruments (hence Dewey's **instrumentalism**) to be used in the attempt to solve problems. In *Reconstruction in Philosophy* (1920), Dewey maintained that knowing is intelligent doing. Knowing, in other words, moves from pure contemplation to the business of living. Since we are social beings, knowledge requires a community of knowers who feel a sense of satisfaction as unbiased inquirers into the use and value of hypotheses in solving real-life problems.

Because knowledge in science grows through a community of scientists and because Dewey saw science and scientific method as applicable to ethics and social issues, his view was that free and open discussion of ideas, the ability to consider any and all ideas and theories as potential solutions to problems, ought to be given the opportunity for experiment to provide an option among competing ideas. This, too, is the way in which Dewey saw the progress of democratic institutions in the social and political spheres.

PRAGMATISTS ON RELIGION, ETHICS, AND THE SOCIAL WORLD

The Pragmatist's views about knowledge and reality are not separable from positions on the "truths" of religion, ethics, and social and political concerns because the rejection of fixity and finality in knowledge affects views and actions in all realms. James, Dewey, and Rorty are the most vocal exponents of Pragmatism in religion, ethics, and social facets of our lives. This is not to say that the other Pragmatists had nothing to say about these issues, and in fact James had very much to say about religion.

One of William James' most often read works is "The Will to Believe." People often compare this work with the position put forth in "**Pascal's Wager**." Pascal proposed that there are benefits in assenting to the claim that God exists. Pascal's position was that it is always in a person's best interest to believe in God since the alternative is to lose the benefit of belief in this life, and in the worst case where the person does not believe and there is a God, it earns the non-believer a very hot seat in an unbearable eternal existence. James recognized the appeal of Pascal's argumentation, but Pascal's view is filled with veiled threats and cold calculation regarding the status of reward in belief and punishment or unhappiness for disbelief. James wished to go beyond these sorts of reasons to something that would justify belief even when rational or calculated reasons are not taken into account. There are important differences, therefore, between Pascal's betting on God's existence and James' view of the vital good that can accrue to a person in belief – and even in non-belief.

What is important in the question whether we believe in the existence of God and adhere to a religion is not whether we find rational proof of the existence of that being. It is instead that we ought to make a decision based on feelings and desires. We cannot prove God's existence in some abstractly rational fashion; but we can live our lives as though God exists. If a life is made meaningful or better by belief, then so much the better for us and belief in the existence of God. Even if "God" is an abstraction, James has no real objection to it just so long as an abstraction "gets you somewhere." Where it leads depends on the force of the option – to the individual – between belief and non-belief. Like Peirce, James saw that the comfort of belief is important. It is not a matter of complacency or intellectual laziness; belief for a believer is important in living a better life.

James' view is that when we have an **option** for belief, we need to take into account the nature of the option. The option is to believe in God or not to believe. Some options put before us are trivial, avoidable, and essentially dead. In the twenty-first century, belief in the existence of Thor is not really an option. If there are people who believe in and pray to Thor, they are few and far between. For the rest of us, the option is trivial. It is avoidable because there are other potential gods in whom we might believe and so do not feel forced to choose this one and the option is therefore dead. On the other hand, being presented with the possibility that there is a loving, all-powerful, all-knowing God may be appealing and have life-altering consequences. If I am asked whether I would like to convert to Judaism, I see the possibility of doing so as live (there is such a religion), forced (I need to choose to convert or choose not to convert), and I cannot avoid deciding. If I choose to convert to Judaism, it is because I find some vital good in it. I may believe that it will allow me to live my life in ways different from and perhaps better than they are now. This is all the justification for belief anyone needs. Having access to or believing that some particular argument for God's existence is valid has little or nothing to do with the good that belief may provide. There are those for whom religious belief does not offer a vital good and they choose not to believe. That is, like the choice to believe, up to the individual and not something to be rationally determined by considering the quality of arguments for God's existence or threats and calculations concerning points to be "won" in Pascal's game of chance.

Another issue closely related to religious belief and to metaphysical disputes is the question whether our wills are free or determined. James' answer to the question, in typical Pragmatist fashion, is to note that the question really has no answer. But that does not stop us from inquiring into the issue and determining what the consequences of belief one way or the other might be.

A hard determinist, or **fatalist**, contends that there is fixity and finality in the universe with respect to the past, present, and future. The determinist, in short, believes in a mechanistic view in which there is an ultimate explanation of things, whether it is an explanation by cause-and-effect relationships in the natural world or by the mind of God knowing and directing everything. In either case, the result is the same: everything happens as it must, and we have no choice in the matter.

The **indeterminist**, however, holds with the doctrine of chance – that sometimes, things just happen. Neither the indeterminist nor the hard determinist can prove either theory is true. Constantly thinking about it and trying to figure out which of these ways of looking at the relationship between our actions and the world amounts, in short, to spinning our wheels and going nowhere. The point is to find out what difference it makes if we think we are free.

How do we decide the issue of freedom? For James, it is that whatever view regarding the determination (or lack of determination) of the will gives our lives more zest, hope, and excitement is the one we ought to adopt. There is no real benefit in believing that the will is determined by God or by anything else. Believing that our wills are determined makes the universe out to be nothing more than a machine and we are only machines inside of that with lives having no meaning. What is worse logically, however, is that determinism is inconsistent with what we actually think and do. We often regret that things have occurred. Regret is at odds with the will's determination right from the start. As James explained, we regret that certain things have happened, but if no action is anything but what has already been pre-determined in the workings and plan of the world, then judgments of regret are completely irrational and useless. This is especially true in a case in which a person is both a determinist and a theodicist.

A theodicist believes either that evil does not exist at all and we are mistaken about evil's existence or evil does exist but it always works out for the best. In "The **Dilemma of Determinism**" (1895), James explained that if we accept the theodicist's claim that everything ultimately works out for the best, then what are we to make of judgments made in the face of occurrences we believe are bad or evil? If we say some specific action or event should not have been undertaken or should not have occurred, then we are saying that we think things should not work out for the best. Thinking that things should not turn out for the best is incompatible with the view that whatever works out for the best is more acceptable than what does not. This means, then, that the determinist-theodicist might say that what happened was the best, and if it happens that the occurrence was something hideous, like the murder of an innocent person, the determinist-theodicist ends by saying that it is good that an innocent person was murdered. In either case, there is something drastically wrong with belief in determinism of the will because murder cannot be bad without regret being good. Regret cannot be good without murder being bad. Regret simply makes no sense for a determinist.

With this simple distinction in hand between **judgments of regret** and goodness in the universe of the theodicist, the determinist's world makes no sense because the notion of what ought to be the case is meaningless. Things simply are what they are. For the pragmatically minded James, however, there is a simple but elegant solution: choose the free will option because it is more consistent with actual lived behavior involving judgments of regret and what we consider to be moral goodness. To choose determinism might appear at first glance to ensure that the world makes perfectly good sense, but in practical application, it is quite the contrary. James indicates at the end of "The Dilemma of Determinism" that it is important to realize that there is little or no "zest" or "excitement" in a deterministic world, and for him, it is better to take the road of free will than that of determinism for the conduct of real lives in this world.

William James' Pragmatism applied to theological notions such as free will and the option to believe in the existence of God is, like his moral views, centered on the individual's life and what will make it significant for each person. Ethics is a realm in which life's significance takes center stage. For James, there is no ethical system set up in advance. Once we do set one up, it cannot be a dogmatic, fixed ethical system. If there is no final truth in ethics, our highest moral goal, if there is any at all, is to break rules that no longer work to solve problems in the actual conditions of life. We ought to work toward creating the most good possible. How to do this is outlined, at least in part, in two of James's works in ethics, "What Makes a Life Significant" (1891) and "The Moral Philosopher and the Moral Life" (1891).

James clarified the importance in ethics of one's own point of view. Socially, we do not raise monuments to people in the working class because we tend to think that they have done nothing important and have no **ideals**. For James, however, ideals are novelties for people who have them; and sometimes simply getting out of the gutter is ideal enough for the unfortunate person who happens to be in it. To think that other people do not have ideals involves the danger inherent in judging others. Judging is dogmatizing about others' ideals and, for James, it is the cause of most injustice and cruelty.

It is inappropriate to judge the life of another or to think the goals and dreams of others are droll or whimsical fantasies. The ideal of one is the banality of another. People who live quiet and comfortable lives, resting easily in their social positions, may have lives and ideals much less interesting and important than construction workers who risk life and limb in building skyscrapers, or the dream of a starving child simply to have enough to eat.

Interestingly, James also noted that comfort is more dangerous than physical danger and that society itself will be much improved if we work toward maintaining the "**martial virtues**" even while we seek to end all war. In "The Moral Equivalent of War" (1906) James inveighed against war as something that may some day be outlawed. Even so, he argued that to preserve the zest for life, to continue to improve and progress, we must retain military discipline in fearlessness, strength, power, and other-regarding interests that are the foundation upon which states are built. Reflective people ought to notice that those who live lives the complete opposite of poor laborers no more deserve comfort than the poor and the working class deserve toil and hardship. James did not suggest that everyone toil incessantly in dirt, grime, and pain, but instead that we all should experience what it is to work and develop the kind of toughness possessed by the working class. It would build a better world of united communities working toward a common goal.

Dewey's conception of the nature of values revolves around his view of scientific hypotheses and the influence of Darwin's theory on philosophy. The theory of evolution transforms the world of knowledge, showing that metaphysical speculations are impractical. The theory of evolution also leads away from absolutism. For Dewey, we make progress possible with hypotheses formulated to understand and live in the world, but we do not create hypotheses and theories expecting that they will end in fixed and final solutions to all human problems. Just as scientific hypotheses are subject to revision and to being discarded, moral and social hypotheses are to be treated like means to an end where the end is to solve practical problems.

Method in ethics and method in science are practically the same in the sense that the scientist does not figure out whether a theory of science is true by comparing it with an ultimate standard – and neither does the ethicist. In the same way that we do not expect an architect to find help in constructing a building by consulting an abstract idea of "building," in the moral realm having some ante-cedently determined notion of the abstraction called "good" might be useful, at best, in realizing that there is a good to be sought and obligations to be met. But "good" is practical, concrete, lived experience, not an abstraction.

There are no final ends in ethics and society. The ends we have in view are always provisional. Dewey's position was that people should be as ashamed of themselves to say that they follow or are loyal to a principle in ethics because some philosopher proposed it as they would be to say that they accept a theory in physics because of their respect or reverence for Isaac Newton. We use and test ideas to find out how well they work in solving practical problems. If they are successful, if they work or they "will do" to get us by, they are appropriate for respect. Dewey found it amazing that people fight wars over the truth of theories, religions, morals, and politics when what they ought to do is simply put them to the test of action to find out whether they work in practice.

Dewey found absolutist religious views just as absurd. People absolutely devoted to an absolute creed or religious value system tend to look with a jaundiced eye on social values because they are created by humans rather than by God. Absolutists tend to devalue personal relationships because they are not as important as our relationship to God and religion. In fact, Dewey said, social values and family values are considered to be "dangerous rivals of higher values" because they offer strong temptations to revolt against the word of God. So instead of embracing this world's values, beings, and things, an absolutist religious doctrine is more likely to lead toward devaluing the world of humanity in favor of an abstract world in which we do not live. Dewey's suggestion is that the values we hold in this world are verified or tested by experimental means to determine whether they "work," whether they "will do," and we would be better off concentrating attention on this-worldly values for effective and real change in this world.

The same considerations apply to our social and political lives. Ethics is experimental, like the sciences, and is tested in part by free and open inquiry and discussion. Because of its social character and openness, it is a method of democracy. The opposite of this is to appeal to authority, tradition, and precedent, to appeal to what stifles creativity and silences voices. Dewey did not believe that precedents, authority, and tradition are to be thrown away completely, but he thought they are to be used and not simply followed. This attitude toward the changing nature of theories and principles – that they are to be abandoned when they come up against anomalies of a significant sort for which the theories and principles cannot provide an account – is to be replaced in a revolutionary, scientific way much like that described later by Thomas Kuhn in *The Structure of Scientific Revolutions* (1962).

There are events or policies we consider socially evil that ought neither to exist nor to be put in place. But social evils do not exist because of "human nature" making them inevitable. It is simply that human action is the result of habits developed in solving problems. In cases in which there is an evil in the social realm arising as a result of habits, it is possible to alter habits. This does not necessitate wild revolutionary approaches in the social order, but it does tell us that to effect change, we should look to education for new habits. In the realm of freedom, rights, and justice, we need, in short, to put our conceptions to the test to determine whether they achieve our goals. If they do not, we need to work together to find the solution to problems associated with them.

In government we need to test our conceptions of what is good, true, or right. In *The Public and Its Problems* (1927), Dewey noted that the state is nothing more than the association of people protecting their interests with elected representatives. There is therefore no preconceived rule to establish and follow to create a good state because there is never the same public in different times and places. In other words, Dewey closely approximates the contentions of Paine and Jefferson that every generation has the right to start anew in political life. The public is always different in different ages. Dewey expressed even more clearly than did the American revolutionaries that political fixity, absolute government, or what Robert Nozick would later call "**patterned principles of justice**" that are considered in some way sacred and untouchable, are more likely to result in revolt and revolution than more orderly and directed change. In this view of the possibilities for leading to revolution that Pragmatism entails, George Santayana, also a Pragmatist, noted in "Public Opinion" (1920) that it is not public opinion that leads to revolutions; it is that those who are reformers are a "symptom" of the public disease to which the revolution refers. In this sense, perhaps, American Pragmatism is as revolutionary as the ideas of the founders of the new American republic who thought the disease of tyranny would be cured by American revolutionary thought and action. Perhaps they were right. True democratic institutions are built and sustained in being organized around recognition and acceptance of change and difference, being amenable to different voices and views, and willing to incorporate them into the changing landscape that is not only the American experience, but the human experience everywhere.

RICHARD RORTY AND TWENTIETH-CENTURY AMERICAN PRAGMATISM

Rorty's Pragmatism builds from Deweyan developments of the mid-twentieth century. Rorty, however, sees his philosophical project in a shared predicament that should lead us to feel **solidarity** with others. In feeling solidarity with all people, we will be able to create something better than we now have in our moral, social, and political lives.

Rortyan Pragmatism touches on epistemology, metaphysics, religion, ethics, and politics. The real point in speculation is to make substantive changes to eliminate cruelty and absolutism. Rorty recognized, as Dewey did before him, that everything in the world of experience, from truth to morals to politics, is a product of the vagaries of time and change. In the end, Rorty's **liberal ironist** tendencies are found in his steadfast and resolute contention that we ought to remove cruelty from the world, and he holds steadfastly and resolutely to this even while recognizing that he has absolutely no rational arguments to support the claim. That, however, is no reason to abandon the conviction. With more irony, it is not even possible to prove that being a liberal ironist is better than being anything else – say, a conservative literalist; but Rorty has hope, at least, that liberal irony might provide us a chance for happiness where other points of view have failed.

Rorty's position on the status of knowledge and reality is complicated. As he argued in *Philosophy and the Mirror of Nature* (1979), traditional philosophical systems were designed on and derived from the notion that our minds are capable of representation of the world as it "really is." There are obvious problems with this view that appear in an earlier section of this chapter; but there is the additional complication from developments in twentieth-century analytic philosophy in which philosophical analysts tried to figure out the real nature of things by clarifying words and concepts rather than getting down to the business of philosophy.

At its best, "knowledge" is a description of human behavior. Rorty said his goal was to try to show the way in which the things Dewey and James said about truth would help to replace an "unsatisfactory" present with a better future, and in the process, replace certainty from theories of the past with hope for the future. It is a tall order, but not one we would be well advised to avoid in a world of cruelty and despair. To reach this goal, Rorty recognized that just as there are many different kinds of statements in many different realms of experience and inquiry, there are many different kinds of truths. There are truths in science and literature, truths in engineering and medicine, and the methods of science cannot be applied to all of these in the same way since they are all different ways of conceiving of the world and its problems.

Because many different vocabularies and theories are incommensurable, they are, Rorty says, "right" or "applicable" within their own spheres of influence. The charge of not being a systematic philosopher due to this claim failed to bother Rorty, who thought there were no essences and that the entire world in which we live is a matter of contingency and chance. If there are no eternal essences accessible to us, if all things are contingent, then the meaning of life, as William James made clear, is for us to create. This is, for Rorty, a matter of telling our own stories and being our own persons. This may appear to be a statement of extreme individualism reminiscent of New England Transcendentalists who said we ought to be self-reliant individuals who have no need or use for the rest of society and can become authentic selves by being as far as possible from the crowd, from the cities, and from the cacophonous din of society in which we live. This is not the case for Rorty, who affirms that we are social beings who live in communities, and because this is the case what is important is that we find and build solidarity between and among ourselves, not aimlessly theorize about human nature and ultimate truth. We recognize suffering in the world and it should be alleviated. We have an obligation to alleviate it. It is as simple as that.

Like Dewey, Rorty contended that there are no facts in the world to which we can turn our attention to find out what kinds of communities to form or to determine exactly what we ought to do in every conceivable case to relieve suffering and participate in solidarity with others, but it is possible to engage in discussion to find out what points and experiences we have in common. Doing this is a matter of political freedom making us even more aware of the contingency of our individual and social existences.

It is perhaps the case that Rorty completes Dewey for our entrance into the twenty-first century, giving the distinctively American philosophy of Pragmatism an identifiable and definite goal of its own. The goal is recognizing that what we share with all other human beings is the ability to sympathize with their pain, and that we have an obligation to do just that.

CRITICISMS OF PRAGMATISM

The Pragmatic quest for a workable and reasonable conception of truth has led to the realization that human knowledge is tentative and that previous theories have not only failed to deliver on promises of knowledge, a grasp on the nature of reality, and the promise of a good life in utilizing some a priori theory of everything, but previous theories may contribute to the exact opposite results they are designed to achieve. In this, Pragmatism has provided a valuable service in heightening our sensitivity about and creating in us healthy hesitation in accepting any theory that claims to encompass all things and provide one pre-conceived solution to all of our problems. We should hesitate to adopt them, at the very least, because they create more problems than they solve.

In addition, for those who have respect for the sciences and their practical value, that Pragmatism employs science in philosophy may very well be one of its strongest and most laudable traits. On the other hand, there is a downside in some ways of conceiving of Pragmatism. Pragmatists like William James, for example, say that determinism fails to give meaning to life. But is this necessarily or even likely the case? It is possible to argue the opposite, that true meaning is given by lives being planned in some fashion to reach an ultimate goal, and that if the Pragmatist is right that there is no plan and no goal for the world or for us, then it might lead to despair and depression rather than the zest and excitement in life that James was convinced would be the result. Perhaps some find zest and excitement in life in being a player in a previously written script, and for whom joy is experienced in being part of something larger and more significant than humanity. James also made the comment that soft determinism (compatibilism) is nothing more than what people adopt when they claim to understand hard determinism, but this seems unfair to the theory. Perhaps it is the more rational solution to the fact of causation in the world as well as our adamantly felt feeling that we are free.

Since Pragmatism's use and value are in practical consequences of actions and beliefs, like utilitarianism and its requirement that what is good is what produces the greatest happiness for the greatest number, we are not equipped to know with any reliability what the long-term results of our actions might be. Pragmatism centering on results may be misguided because the results we see as a consequence of experiments at some given time may be at odds with consequences found later, offering no means over time to know what we should do.

It may be that the Pragmatist insisting that the methods of science are applicable to all philosophical topics is false. Even though the Pragmatist rejects the fact/value distinction as "just another dualism," rejecting a position because one does not have evidence that it is true is not the same as having evidence that it is not true. The Pragmatist, however, does realize this distinction and simply retreats to something like the Kantian conception of **antinomies of pure reason** such that there are equally good arguments in both directions on controversial issues and claims, and if the arguments are equally good, perhaps we ought to stop arguing about the issues and satisfy ourselves with what we can do with one or the other, or perhaps even both, of the competing claims.

It is often the case that Pragmatism is considered a "relativistic" theory of truth and morality and because of the common knee-jerk reaction to that accusation, people who are driven toward fixity, finality, and absolute truth will discard the claims of Pragmatism, charging that it is a theory giving itself to any idea that happens to "work" or be "useful" at any given time. While this is actually the case, it is not clear that it is a fair or consistent critical evaluation of Pragmatism since those who would discard the claims of Pragmatism's "true because it is useful" approach to knowledge and morality will accept it for their own theory for the same reasons.

In all, it may be that the strength of Pragmatism is that it recognizes weaknesses. The Pragmatist does not claim that fixity, finality, and the absolute are the goals of the system or of its practitioners, so to dismiss the theory on the basis of the criticism that it fails to lead to "Truth" and "Goodness" and "Perfection" is to beg the question. The Pragmatist never argues that application of Pragmatic method will lead to any such thing as certainty or perfection, so to criticize it on the basis of its failure to do so is to assume the critic's point in question, leaving it both as the reason and the conclusion in the argument to reject Pragmatism out of hand.

CONCLUSION

American Pragmatism embodies the themes of this book. Pragmatism is practical; it puts central focus on change and reform and on revolution in the way in which we do philosophy; and the Pragmatists' quest for meaning in human life is in the ideals of justice, rights, equality, and concern for the suffering of others.

For Pragmatists, change is simply change. We need to learn to deal with it. People who fear (and therefore detest) change are, like Plato, mistaken about what the world in which we live is like. There are changes; there is nothing to disparage in **mutation**. We are not eternal beings and the world is constantly changing. Realizing this is much like Emerson's realization that the soul becomes, and that this really annoys absolutists. Perhaps some conclusions we might reach regarding the Pragmatists are that we need to get a grip on the fact that things around us (and we) are constantly changing and that to retreat into an imaginary world of fixity and perfection to get away from change and contingency is intellectually suspect and morally indefensible. One does not deal with the world by trying to escape from it in eternity and perfection and, if Dewey and Rorty are right about the tendencies of absolutisms of all kinds, absolutism may make this world a less pleasant and inviting place to be. If it is "true" that absolutism is not the solution to our problems but is instead a major contributing factor to their genesis and continued existence, so much the better for us when we abandon absolutism and embrace contingency; and so much the worse for the absolutist because change happens. Pragmatists embrace change as it occurs and they work for change intended to improve our lives. Rorty said in *Philosophy and Social Hope* that America is an example of the best kind of society so far invented even if it has experienced past and present atrocities and it elects people of questionable intelligence and character to high office. If this is the conclusion to be reached through Pragmatism, it is no wonder that Pragmatism is the most distinctly American philosophy in the Western philosophical tradition. It celebrates the democratic spirit. It recognizes difference and diversity. In its best moments it treats all human beings with dignity and value. And in its ideals and aspirations, it is a place in which, for the Pragmatist at least, we can find ways to alleviate suffering, promote equality, and provide the chance for all human beings to start their lives with a chance to be happy.

FURTHER READING

Excellent works on American Pragmatism include: Ruth Anna Putnam, ed., *The Cambridge Companion to William James* (New York: Cambridge University Press, 1997); Molly Cochran, ed., *The Cambridge Companion to Dewey* (New York, Cambridge University Press, 2010), and Cheryl J. Misak, ed., *The Cambridge Companion to Peirce* (New York: Cambridge University Press, 2004). On Rorty, see Christopher J. Voparil and Richard J. Bernstein, ed., *The Rorty Reader* (Malden, MA: Blackwell, 2010). There are excellent resources on American Pragmatism at www.pragmatism.org.

7

RECENT DEVELOPMENTS IN AMERICAN PHILOSOPHY

PART I

This chapter and Chapter 8 are centered on recent developments in American philosophy beyond the Pragmatists. Because the number of American philosophers working in the twentieth and twenty-first centuries is exceptionally large and their areas of concentration are broad and far-reaching, Chapter 7 covers metaphysics, epistemology, philosophy of science, philosophy of religion with special attention to the unity of Native American philosophy while Chapter 8 is devoted to ethics, social philosophy, and political philosophy.

There is significant and important revolutionary work in the recent past having a pragmatic connection in metaphysics, epistemology, and philosophy of science. In metaphysics and epistemology, the works of Willard Van Orman Quine and Edmund Gettier take pride of place. In philosophy of science, Thomas Kuhn's groundbreaking *The Structure of Scientific Revolutions* suits exceptionally well the revolutionary theme of this book. Further, a look at the unity of Native American philosophy will highlight the important, long overdue, and recent inclusion of Native American philosophy in mainstream American thought that appears in only a few books on American philosophy.

METAPHYSICS, EPISTEMOLOGY, AND PHILOSOPHY OF SCIENCE

W. V. O. Quine (1908–2000) is one of the most important philosophers in the twentieth century. He worked primarily in epistemology and the philosophy of science. Quine challenged the traditional **analytic/synthetic distinction** and he is well-known for his work on **naturalized epistemology**. There is nothing easy about Quine's work, but a step toward clarification begins with the traditional epistemological distinction between **analytic and synthetic statements** to which Quine takes exception in "Two Dogmas of Empiricism" (1953).

Beginning primarily with Immanuel Kant, epistemologists tended to make a rigid distinction between analytic and synthetic statements. Analytic statements are true by definition or by virtue of the meaning of their terms and are true independently of experience. In other words, the concept of the subject of an analytic statement is pre-contained in the concept of the predicate (e.g., "All bachelors are unmarried men") and they are necessarily true. Synthetic statements are verified by experience and are those whose subject terms are "amplified" by their predicates such that the concept of the predicate is not pre-contained in the concept of the subject (e.g., "All bachelors are under nine feet tall"). Quine, however, doubts the accuracy of this representation of the nature of statements because the status of analytic statements is not as clear as logical positivists and philosophical analysts believe it is.

If we ask what it means for terms to be synonymous, we may look to their interchangeability or to a lexicographer's statement that they "mean the same thing," but that is exactly the point in question. The essence of analyticity is synonymy, but synonymy means analyticity, so we are nowhere near clarification of the meaning of the notion of an "analytic" statement. As Quine explained, the notion that there is a distinction between these statements is "an unempirical dogma" and a matter of metaphysical faith. Since the logical positivists claim that any statement that is not verifiable either in fact or in principle by experience is meaningless, Quine's criticism shows that their distinction between the analytic and the synthetic, which they use to reject many metaphysical and theological statements as meaningless and insignificant, applies also to their system of thought.

Quine adds that the second dogma of empiricism is reductionism. Reductionism is the claim that for any synthetic statement, there are experiences whose addition makes the truth of the synthetic statement more likely and there are other experiences whose addition makes the truth less likely. For Quine, the case is not so simple. Verification (or falsification) of a view is more than the simple accumulation of observations for one side or the other. Like the Pragmatists, Quine contends there are times when an anomalous or particularly vexing experience may be so momentous and important that we need to change our previous beliefs regarding a statement or theory. Or, in other words, statements and theories become true, in James' way of putting the case, and it is the court of experience and the usefulness of our claims to truth that make all the difference.

Just as he rejected the dualism of the analytic/synthetic distinction, Quine approached epistemology from the point of view of experience in establishing claims to truth. The history of Western philosophy from Plato to David Hume and the logical positivists is alive with references to our inability to "know" a world distinct from our impressions or experiences. Plato expressed the point in the **Allegory of the Cave** where human beings always fall short of the quest for knowledge of things as they actually are because we are trapped in a world of sense experience. John Locke admitted that "**sensitive knowledge**" fell short of the certainty of **intuition** and **demonstration**, and Hume showed that claims regarding the external world are only about "impressions" and "ideas" and not about the things themselves. Kant took the issue further than Hume in stating that humans possess categories of the understanding through which experience is organized. This means it really does not matter whether the world as it actually is — which we cannot know because it is the noumenal world — is as we perceive it. What we have are phenomena and our intellectual processes. And that is all.

Quine's view takes its lead from the inability of philosophers to "prove" the existence of an external world and, as a result, find themselves in all kinds of epistemological quandaries. In place of epistemology caught between lack of sufficient proof of an external world and an equally persistent conviction that there is one, Quine proposes "naturalized epistemology," the position that since all we have for evidence of an external world is sense experiences, we should "settle for psychology." This means that we would be better off to think of epistemology as we think of science, and indeed think of epistemology as a branch of science. If epistemology is a branch of science, epistemologists will focus their attention on how people move from mere sense experiences to belief in a world of transcendent things. They would not speculate about knowledge of an external world that is forever beyond our philosophical and scientific reach. If epistemologists followed Quine's lead, many of the problems of epistemology about the distinction between the knower and the known would dissolve. Perhaps it would be like the Deweyan view of the status of many, if not most, of our philosophical problems once a practical approach is taken to them: we would not solve those problems, we would *get over them*.

Edmund Gettier (1927–), in "Is **Justified True Belief** Knowledge?" (1963) challenged the traditional definition of "knowledge" that had held since Plato. The conception of knowledge addressed by Gettier's work is the contention that we have knowledge of "P" (a proposition or statement) when three conditions obtain. They are that (1) the statement, P, is true, (2) the knowing subject believes that P is true, and (3) the knowing subject is justified in believing that P is true. Gettier's challenge to the traditional account of knowledge is in showing that it is possible to satisfy all three of the conditions for knowledge but still not be in possession of knowledge.

Consider this overview of the Gettier examples. The first example is about two people, Smith and Jones, who have applied for the same job. Smith believes (and is justified in believing by virtue of information provided to him) that Jones will get the job and that Jones has ten coins in his pocket. Smith concludes that the man with ten coins in his pocket will get the job. It turns out to be true that the man with ten coins in his pocket will get the job. But the person who gets the job is Smith, not Jones. Smith, in concluding that the man with ten coins in his pocket would get the job, was right – but he was not right about who would get the job since he (Smith) got the job and Smith *also* has ten coins in his pocket. So Smith believed that the man with ten coins in his pocket would get the job, he was justified in believing it, and what he justifiably believed was true. But Smith did not possess knowledge.

The second Gettier example is about one man's claim to knowledge regarding ownership of a car by Jones and the location of another man, Brown. Smith has evidence that Jones owns a Ford. Assume that the source of and evidence about Jones' ownership of a Ford are reliable. Now, take into account that if the statement "P" (Jones owns a Ford) is true, then the statement "P or Q" is also true. Smith does not know the location of Brown, but he asserts

the following: "Either Jones owns a Ford or Brown is in Barcelona."
Even though Smith does not have any information regarding the
location of Brown, the statement regarding Jones' ownership and
Brown's location is necessarily true regardless of whether Brown is
in Barcelona. Interestingly enough, it turns out that Jones does *not*
own a Ford even though all the evidence pointed to his ownership.
Now, what is the status of the statement that "Either Jones owns a
Ford or Brown is in Barcelona"?

It is impossible at this point to tell whether the statement "Either
Jones owns a Ford or Brown is in Barcelona" is true because for a
disjunction (an "either-or" statement) to be true, at least one disjunct
must be true. All we know is that "Jones owns a Ford" is false. If
Brown really is in Barcelona, the statement is true even though
Jones does not own a Ford. If Brown really is not in Barcelona, the
statement is false since we now know that "Jones owns a Ford" is
false (and again, a simple disjunction is false only when both dis-
juncts are false). One may, at this point, declare that the status of
the original statement is unknown. Given the conditions in the
example, however, this clearly is not the case. Even though Smith
had no evidence about the location of Brown, it turns out that
Brown is, in fact, in Barcelona. Oddly enough, on the traditional
conception of knowledge as justified true belief, once we discover
that Brown is in Barcelona, and even though Jones does not in fact
own a Ford, Smith is still justified in believing the entirety of the
statement "Either Jones owns a Ford or Brown is in Barcelona"
since the statement is true, Smith is justified in believing it,
and Smith does believe it to be the case.

What are the implications of the Gettier Problem? First are some
practical considerations. Many philosophers have tried to overcome
the Gettier Problem by showing that there is something wrong
with the examples used. Others have approached the problem by
noting that if the three traditional criteria for knowledge are insufficient, we should attempt to find a fourth criterion that will solidify
claims to knowledge. Others have argued for clarification of the
original three criteria. No matter which approach one takes, however, Gettier has offered a serious challenge to the traditional and
long-standing philosophical definition of knowledge. In any case,
the Gettier Problem may offer more reason to adopt a Pragmatist
point of view that it is not the justification of absolute truth that

matters, but what we do with our claims to truth. So if there is some concrete difference made in believing and claiming to know that the man with ten coins in his pocket got the job, then the Gettier Problem makes a difference. If, for example, Smith, who believed that the man with ten coins in his pocket who got the job was Jones and not himself, decided to commit suicide on the basis of his derivative "knowledge" that he (Smith) did not get the job, then we should concern ourselves with the problem of knowledge justification raised by the Gettier Problem. But if the point is, as it seems to be in most of the history of Western philosophy, simply another philosophical preoccupation with absolute truth, the Gettier Problem, for the Pragmatist, is a difference that makes no difference.

Thomas Kuhn (1922–96) is, like Quine and Gettier, exceptionally influential in philosophy all over the world. His work is arguably the most far-reaching and significant in the philosophy of science in America. In *The Structure of Scientific Revolutions*, Kuhn challenges the widely held view that scientific progress and knowledge proceed in an orderly, rational, and cumulative fashion.

Science, as it is practiced, is **normal science**. Normal science is the day-to-day work of scientific practitioners who go about developing medicines, testing theories, and doing experiments. Kuhn explains that normal science does not aim at novelty except insofar as science may lead to the cure for a disease or tell us something about plants, rocks, humans, or any other part of the natural universe we did not know before. But with respect to the scientific enterprise itself, there are no surprises. Scientists use methods, experiments, and observations to increase knowledge and to provide technical solutions to worldly problems.

Normal science thus conducted proceeds according to a **paradigm**. The scientific paradigm is the scientific worldview and methods its practitioners use to increase knowledge and advance solutions to problems. Generally speaking, normal science proceeds with little in the way of disruptions in techniques or observations. Occasionally, as Kuhn notes, the paradigm experiences a crisis brought about by an **anomaly**.

In the conduct of normal science, the appearance of an anomaly does not usually and automatically lead to rejection of an already accepted theory or scientific world view, but if a sufficient number of anomalies occur or if one very significant anomaly arises in the conduct of normal science that normal science cannot solve, a new paradigm (i.e., a new scientific view or theory) will take the place of the current theory or paradigm. The replacement of one paradigm with another is a **scientific revolution**.

It is important to note that scientific revolutions, like Jefferson's political revolution in America, do not take place for "light and transient causes" and they do not take place if there is nothing with which to replace the problematic theory or paradigm. If there is a new paradigm of science already proposed at the time of the occurrence of an anomaly, or if a new paradigm is developed as a result of the occurrence of an anomaly that is sufficiently significant to lead to the development of the new paradigm, it is then that a scientific revolution takes place. This all sounds very simple, but it is much more complex than this brief description of the occurrence of a scientific revolution shows.

While there are rules for the conduct of science, and the rules determine the practice of science, it is the creative and considered judgments of the practitioners of science that determine when anomalous occurrences, experiences, or observations lead to the justification for **paradigm shift**. The paradigm in which practitioners of science operate is not coextensive with rules; instead, the paradigm is more than its rules and procedures. The community of scientists is the deciding factor in whether a paradigm shift (scientific revolution) ought to take place. They determine this through discussion based on experience in scientific practice and using considered judgments, both by using or referring to the rules of competing paradigms and by determining the significance of the different arguments provided on any sides of the issue regarding paradigm change. It is imperative to understand, however, that competing paradigms are incompatible such that each scientific community uses its own paradigm to argue for its paradigm and there is no translation and no commonalities between them. They are, as Kuhn puts it, **incommensurable**.

There is a pragmatic element to Kuhn's description of the progress of science in that it is community-based and that paradigms are ways of conceiving of the world. This seems to mean – and it is consistent with Kuhn's claim that the point of science is not the achievement of truth but to solve puzzles – that the role of science is practical application in the attempt to solve problems. Equally important for understanding Kuhn's position on the nature of normal science and the "structure" of scientific revolutions is that there is no theory that can be subjected to all conceivable tests (just as Quine noted that there is no statement that can be conclusively verified because there is no way in which every conceivable observation about it can be had), and we are mistaken in thinking that a theory has ever been conclusively verified. Instead, we must think in terms of the probability that a paradigm or worldview is true. When it works (i.e., when normal science continues to answer questions posed to it, when it continues to solve puzzles), it is "more" true. When it ceases to work (i.e., when a significant anomaly or group of anomalies confront it), it is "less" true. The community of science determines when the diminished probability of the truth of a paradigm leads to its rejection and subsequent acceptance of a new paradigm that can answer all the questions previously answered by the former paradigm and that can answer the questions or solve the puzzles that the former paradigm could not handle.

Some commentators have applied Kuhn's notion of scientific revolutions and the associated concepts of paradigm, paradigm shift, incommensurability, and normal science to realms other than natural science such as to social sciences and the humanities. Sociologists of science have been particularly interested in Kuhn's work for explaining the nature of communities and for understanding the history of science. Whether the concept of "scientific revolutions" is applicable to realms other than science is beyond the scope of this discussion. The point remains that Kuhn's arguments concerning the history and progress of science constitute a groundbreaking and revolutionary achievement in the philosophy of science.

NATIVE AMERICAN PHILOSOPHY

NATIVE AMERICAN PHILOSOPHY: A PREFATORY NOTE

Before embarking on a discussion of Native American philosophy, it is important to note several features of Native American thought and an important detail regarding me, a white, middle-aged, "native born," secular American woman of Western European descent who is writing about it. Native American philosophy is not "new." It has been in existence as long as there have been Native Americans.

On the other hand, Native American philosophy as an academic discipline is new, having grown only recently (within the past few decades) with the work of Native American philosophers such as Ann Waters, Vine Deloria, Jr. (1933–2005) and Viola Cordova (d. 2002). There are very few books (relatively speaking) on Native American philosophy and even fewer books in American philosophy that make more than vague or passing references to Native American thought, and some make no reference to Native American thought at all. My and Bruce Silver's *Philosophy in America, Volumes I and II* are among those in which Native American philosophy is never mentioned. I rectify the omission in those two books in this book, doing my best to present an accurate picture of Native American philosophy.

Presenting an accurate picture of Native American philosophy, however, may be beyond my ability. If this is so, it is not for lack of trying or of being remiss in reading the works of Native Americans. It is, instead, that I am not an indigenous Native American and I have not and cannot immerse myself in the culture from which the philosophy springs. Because Native American philosophy arises through and from an **oral tradition** and depends on understanding the significance of sacred places, it is not clear that even Native American philosophers can explain their philosophy adequately to others in written form when it is a philosophy that must be lived and embedded in a community. I believe, however, that I have formed a reasonably accurate, even if necessarily incomplete, picture and conception of Native American philosophy from studying their works in the same way that I have read and studied the works of many African American philosophers (I am not African American) and the work of Edwards (I am not a Calvinist man). A problem in attempting to provide some definitive statements about Native American philosophy in a small book on American philosophy in the Western tradition is that non-indigenous philosophers will read Native American thought through the lenses of traditional Western philosophy. I have done this – and many elements of Native American philosophy will be lost in translation of its content by a person steeped only in the Western tradition. I do my best, however, to write with appropriate respect for Native American philosophical traditions and to provide a means by which one may try to understand it through the lenses of the Western tradition.

Deloria pointed out that there is a distinct difficulty even in the Native Americans' attempt to create American Indian philosophy. Western people may believe that tribal traditions are about beliefs and ethnic pride expressed by primitive people and societies. Prejudice against Native thought needs to be obviated by recognizing that while there may be differences in approaches to understanding and being in the world, they are equally legitimate. The notion of equal legitimacy of Native American philosophy is similar to Carol Gilligan's (see Chapter 8) contention that there are differences between male and female ways of conceiving of ethics, but differences do not indicate that one view is superior to another simply in light of the fact that they are different. Non–Native Americans trying to understand the philosophical endeavors of Native Americans may enrich Western philosophy, and that possibility is appealing.

THE UNITY OF NATIVE AMERICAN PHILOSOPHY: AN OVERVIEW

Native American philosophy is distinctly different from most of Western philosophy, and since traditional American philosophy begins with individualistic Enlightenment thought in the Modern era, Native American thought is much different from almost all of traditional European American philosophy. Some of the most important senses in which this is the case regarding Native American philosophy are the following: It arises from an oral tradition of teaching and understanding, it rejects "ultimate causality" or final solutions in understanding and knowledge, it is a view that the Earth is sacred and holy, and that a communal way of life is central to doing and understanding. Because of these features of Native American thought, its epistemology, philosophy of science, metaphysics, ethics, and social thought are interrelated and inseparable.

Traditional European American philosophy depends on the written word and on reason for analysis and understanding. This is not the case for Native American philosophy. Native American philosophy is traditionally told rather than written. It can be told in a variety of ways, including dances, art, stories, and poetry. An essential aspect of understanding it comes about through ways of living, being, knowing, and doing. The philosophy is this–worldly and practical. It's this-worldliness is grounded in the notion that the Earth is Mother. Its practicality is in the refusal of Native American philosophers to occupy themselves with questions about ultimate foundations and ultimate causation.

What matters in Native American thought is our relationship to what exists – that is, all of existence, including the land and other human beings. A communal way of life informs a conception of relatedness and interdependency.

Chief Luther Standing Bear (Oglala Sioux) (1868–1939) said that a primary difference between white and Native people is that the white people see nature as dangerous and seek to dominate it while the Native American believes nature to be accommodating and seeks harmony with it. Thomas Paine is one among very few examples of European Americans who thought of nature in a way similar to that of the Native American, but the few exceptions in traditional Western philosophy do not weaken its general tendency to be predominantly focused on mastery over nature (and of people over each other). And because Western philosophy tends toward a view of human beings as largely isolated rights possessors who are in communities but not fully parts of them, the communal nature of Native American philosophers leads to distinct differences between Native American and traditional European American views of epistemology, metaphysics, religious beliefs and practices, and ethical and social thought and action.

For Native American epistemology and views of science, things are decidedly different from traditional American philosophy in significant ways. The general tendency in European American philosophy has historically been to think of a human knower as an atomistic individual on the model of the Cartesian self who is separated from the contingencies of experience and individual existence to acquire pristine knowledge from a pristine source: pure reason. For Native Americans, knowledge is certainly not gained through pure reason. It is **"embodied" or "lived" knowledge**. This conception of knowledge depends on neither foundations nor abstractions.

In the sense that there are no abstractions or foundations in Native American epistemology, it seems very similar to the Pragmatist's eschewing of dualisms, foundations, and abstractions. A major difference, however, seems to be that Native American philosophy does not grow, as American Pragmatism did, as a reaction to another kind of philosophy that sought abstractions and foundations. Instead, Native American philosophy is practical and concrete in and of itself, not having grown out of a different tradition of thought. Because Native Americans see the practical nature of knowledge from the outset, they have no need to defend their position against any other.

Native American epistemology builds on itself in its communal nature. Note, for example, that Descartes was quite literally removed from all other human beings in the six days it took him to write *Meditations on First Philosophy* and derived the ultimate criterion of truth from the isolated standpoint of the disinterested and unencumbered knower. This conception of the origin of knowledge, with forced hyperbolic doubt as the point at which a quest for supposedly "real" knowledge begins, makes no sense to the Native American philosopher. Instead, the search for knowledge comes from lived experience where questions come to human beings in real experiences.

The Native American way of seeking knowledge precedes Peirce's insistence that Cartesian method and quest are far removed from common practice, usefulness, and the reality of the way ordinary people go about acquiring information. On the other hand, Native American knowledge-seeking is not like Peircean "itch-scratching" and it does not move toward Peirce's attachment to scientific method. Peirce's concept of science is that it is very specialized even if it has a communal flavor to it, but for Peirce it is the community of inquirers using the same scientific method. For the Native American, however, searching for knowledge includes the experiences of everyone, not simply a community of scientific or philosophical inquirers using a formal method.

That knowing involves community and that stringent method is not a requirement for knowing also characterize and inform native conceptions of science. Because nature is constantly changing, it is neither necessary nor possible to think of science on the model of laws and procedures. Native American science is a matter of trying to understand the essences of things. This approach to scientific inquiry seems similar to Jonathan Edwards' implicit goals in the "Spider Letter." Edwards sought scientific understanding because he saw it as a means by which a fuller understanding of the nature and beauty of the universe, and of the work of God in nature, could be conceived.

Those who might say that Native science is not really scientific because it deals with soft considerations such as "beauty" and "feeling" must also consider Edwards' work – which dealt with nearly identical terms and concepts to understand God – as non-scientific. That position would hold, however, only if we consider Isaac Newton to be "unscientific" since Edwards used the principles and procedures of the new science of mechanics of his time and combined it with "a sense of the heart" to achieve more full understanding of the nature, being, and goodness of God. That the Native American seeks relational knowledge does not move the Native view far, if at all, from the Edwardsian conception of understanding (in his case, of God) that transcends mere rational inquiry. Where Edwards was seeking absolute knowledge of ultimate reality and God, however, the Native American is concerned with how to apply knowledge in this world.

The parallel (and it is only a parallel or an analogy) between Edwards' search for knowledge or understanding of God and that of the Native Americans' search for application of knowledge for the here and now is clear. If the most important knowledge for the Native American is knowledge of how to deal with this world, and knowing how to deal with this world requires that we recognize ourselves as dependent upon nature, we are not masters over nature, but are instead dependent on it. In a similar way, one of the results of Edwards' inquiry into the relationship between human beings and God is to show that we are thoroughly, utterly, and necessarily dependent upon God for what we are, what we have, and why we exist at all.

For the Native American philosopher, it is simply the case that what is, is. The ultimate question of metaphysics, "What is real?" is for the Native American simple to answer. Everything that exists is real. There is no need to argue for the existence of some "ultimate" reality. Reality is here and now and all that there is. Cordova, for example, said that the Native American is a monist because the universe is all there is, and it is a given. There is no need, then, to argue for a distinction between appearance and reality or to place one element of what there is in a position of prominence over others.

The nature of reality is inseparable from Native religion. In the same way that there is one and only one universe, and it is what there is, there is no need for postulating a God separate from this world because the world itself exhibits religious importance.

Consistently with Cordova's contention that the Native American is a monist, Native thought provides that God is everywhere. In other words, God is not separate from any other thing. This means, too, that the Native American concepts of religion and morality are inseparably connected such that there is no need to think that there is a God watching over humans. For the Native American, a view of "god" as a vengeful being makes no sense. In a similar way, the Native American does not think about or postulate the existence of some other world that is better (or worse) than this one to which people go after death. Instead, the Earth is where we belong. We come from the Earth and go back to it.

Being from the Earth and returning to it indicates another distinction between traditional Western philosophical and religious views. Western thinkers consider time to be linear and that all things are coming to some grand conclusion. For the Native American, everything is part of a great circle and human lives never really end.

Because Earth is sacred to the Native American, and because Native American religion depends on sacred places and spaces, conflict between the dominant Western culture and Native American religion has been an ongoing problem. Native American children were, up until the early twentieth century, regularly taken from their homes and enrolled in state-run schools with a curriculum designed to erase any and all vestiges of tribal religious beliefs, traditions, and practices. It is ironic that Europeans came to America to escape religious persecution, but it did not keep them from engaging in the same practices from which they sought solace.

Further, the use of public land for Native American religious practice has been hotly contested. Even though despicable and contradictory government policy regarding Native American religion has largely ceased, Native Americans still face obstacles in trying to make the U.S. government understand the need for sacred places and spaces in which to practice tribal religions. The difference for the Native American, compared with Western religious practices, is striking. Where the Christian can put up a church anywhere and create it as a "house of the Lord," the same is not true in Native American religion. Sacredness is tied to places, not simply to practices.

Native American ethics and social thought are united with epistemological, metaphysical, and religious views. It is not possible to separate elements of Native American thought and neatly set them apart from each other as is often done in traditional Western and American philosophy. One way to conceive of this inseparability is to remember that respect is at the foundation of Native American metaphysics (that all things are one and all are equally real) and it is the foundation of Native American ethics. This overriding view in Native thought is that the Earth has given itself to all of us and we are to respect and share it with each other. Because this is the case, caring and sharing are at the center of the Native American communal way of life.

Cordova and other Native American philosophers have noted that there is a similarity between Native American ethics and that of the ancient Greeks. The similarity is at least that humans are naturally social. But the Native American takes the sociability of humanity further than the Greeks in insisting on human equality. The Greeks had no such notion of equality. For Aristotle, for example, the concept of justice rested on believing that equals should get equal shares and unequals should get unequal shares of social goods, and that there are people who are natural masters and others who are natural slaves. There is no such concept of hierarchy in Native American moral thought.

The lack of hierarchical thinking and the acceptance of an inclusive sense of equality is perhaps the essence of Native American ethics. By not accepting hierarchical divisions, the Native American does not see human relationships as processes of bargaining, getting out of each other's way, or as belligerent people competing for scarce resources. The Western contention that we are in competition with each other and make deals with each other to achieve minimal social cooperation is antithetical to the Native American. It is interesting and important to note that in Native American thought, thinking of humans as competitors leads to isolation and selfishness while it is the reverse in Western thought. For example, Hobbes held that isolation and self-interest lead to war, which leads to grudging acceptance of social organization only for the individual's interest. For the Native American, isolation and selfishness are both the cause *and* the effect of thinking of humanity as separate from communities in being non-cooperative and competitive. Unlike the Western philosopher who thinks people are isolated individuals in competition for scarce resources, the Native American thinks that survival depends on cooperation. Further, Native Americans tend to recognize *cooperation as natural* instead of thinking of themselves as individuals separate from community for whom *cooperation is artificial*.

The central place of community in Native American thought also affects understanding of and reaction to wrongdoing. Wrongdoing comes about as a result of failure to realize one's place in the community and disrespecting others. In communitarian Native American societies, banishment from the tribe is an appropriate reaction to wrong done. Since one's humanity is created within the community, there is no more severe punishment for the Native American than to be exiled (i.e., no longer recognized as a human being) from the group.

The Native American's conception of the inherently social nature of humanity provides for a refreshingly different (from Western philosophy) way to understand the human being's relationship to the world and to others. That humans are social beings, having ties to all things, means that Native American understanding of what there is, what we know, who we are, and what we ought to do are intertwined. The Native American's thought is unified, bringing the sacred, the human, the social, and the natural all into one.

While Native Americans continue to experience roadblocks in the way of practicing spiritual, religious, and traditional ways of living and being, they have risen from the ashes of years of suppression to continue building Native American philosophy. Building it benefits the Native American and it may very well benefit traditional Western philosophy. For example, for there to be no heaven and no hell, for there to be nowhere but right here that is reality, may lead the Western believer to wonder what state of the universe is created by this view. The Western believer may think that there is no foundation for morality and no sense of right and wrong. Such a belief, however, could not be further from the truth. Native American metaphysics and philosophy of religion, just like Native American science, epistemology, and ethics, are communal and relational. There is a this-worldly foundation for morality suitable for living a good, moral life that is consistent with the sacredness of the land, of the Earth, of all that is.

CRITICISMS

While Quine was able to illuminate some of the problems with traditional views of knowledge, it is not clear that denying the analytic/synthetic distinction has much practical value beyond admonitions to be more careful in making epistemological claims. In addition, it is perhaps the case that we need not worry ourselves over the question whether "analytic" and "synonymy" are truly the same, or whether there is a fundamental lack of clarity in the issue. It may be that what matters most is what we do with our ideas.

Whether justified true belief is really knowledge is an esoteric problem. It has the capacity to generate intellectual interest and it creates fascinating "Gettier Problems" that often defy solution, but what is the point? Some have also noted that the entire problem may be much ado about nothing. Is it really the case in the history of philosophy that a majority of philosophers have defined the term "knowledge" in the way in which Gettier has expressed it as "justified true belief?" It may be that Gettier defined the "problem" into existence, and the conception of knowledge he claims has characterized the history of Western thought is more a construct of his own than philosophically common.

Native American conceptions of the nature of reality and knowledge are not easily subsumed under the categories in which we often conceive of problems of philosophy in the Western tradition. The claim that Native American philosophy can be taught and expressed only orally ignores the possibility that speaking a position using words, which are symbols of thoughts, is not really much different from writing a philosophical position using words as ink on paper since they, too, are symbols for thoughts. The Native American philosopher tends to believe that there is something lost in their philosophy when non-Native philosophers attempt to write about or understand it, largely and often because the non-Native will do so by using concepts from her or his own tradition and not that of the Native American. It may be, however, that something is lost in the translation of all philosophical positions, whether from the past or in the present, when one is attempting to learn and to express a position different from her own. For example, does the same criticism apply to an American who tries to understand ancient Greek philosophy? It is a good possibility, but this should not keep us from trying to grapple with the issues as we understand them and to make the best use of our understanding of ancient Greek thought here and now. In a similar way, the European American's inability to immerse herself completely in Native American culture and history does not preclude the honest attempt to give it a fair hearing and to make use of it to try to improve the human condition.

The Native American is no more immune to the problems inherent in the clash between individual and community than the European American's problem of grappling with it. While it is true that Native American thought has a particularly communitarian flavor, part of what now affects the expression and acceptance of Native American thought is its contrast with individualistic conceptions of science and knowledge and the place of the individual in the community. In addition, while Native science is a refreshing change from views of science in the Western tradition, it is not clear that application of the concepts presented thus far will be efficacious in solving real-life problems (development of vaccines and technologies, for example) as Western science has been able to realize.

Native American ethics and social thought seem likely to be subject to the same problems and difficulties as traditional virtue-ethics and communitarinism. Even if the Native American is not concerned, like the European American, with individual rights and protecting oneself from encroachments and incursions of others on one's property and person, there is still the danger that difference and development of unique solutions to problems or ways of living will be discouraged within tribes or groups. If there is any truth to the Emersonian notion that it is the peculiar person, the misfit, the one who bucks the system who is likely to be a creator and innovator, Native American ways of life may result in stifled individual creativity and initiative. I think, however, that this is not more likely for the Native American than it is for the European who adopts the view, like that of Aristotle, that the whole is prior to its part or that the state (or group) is prior to the individual.

CONCLUSION

In this chapter we have seen some significant developments in American metaphysics, epistemology, and philosophy of science in the twentieth century. We have also seen the ways in which Native American thought in these realms of philosophical inquiry are distinct from traditional American philosophy especially with respect to their overriding "communitarian" nature. Taking into account the unity of Native American philosophy in its concentration on the centrality of community in metaphysical, epistemological, scientific, religious, and moral realms provides a useful transition and point of important contrast to further developments in twentieth- and twenty-first-century American philosophy in ethics, social, and political thought.

FURTHER READING

There is an enormous number of resources on the topics of this chapter. Some accessible and useful ones covering a broad range of topics are: Alex Orenstein, *V.W. Quine* (Princeton: Princeton University Press, 2002); Noah Lemos, *An Introduction to the Theory of Knowledge* (New York: Cambridge University Press, 2007); Gary Gutting, *Paradigms and Revolution* (Notre Dame: University of Notre Dame Press, 1980); and Imre Lakatos, ed., *Criticism and the Growth of Knowledge* (Cambridge: Cambridge Uuniversity Press, 1970).

On Native American philosophy, exceptional original sources include V. F. Cordova, *How It Is* (Tucson: University of Arizona Press, 2007) and Vine Deloria, Jr., *God is Red: A Native View of Religion* (New York: Putnam, 1973); Deloria has written several books on other aspects of Native American thought including science, political theory, and higher education. Ann Waters' *American Indian Thought: Philosophical Essays* (Malden, MA: Blackwell, 2004) is an important collection of essays by Native Americans. An excellent source of information on Native American Philosophy is the *American Philosophical Association's Newsletter on American Indians in Philosophy* available at www.apaonline.org.

8

RECENT DEVELOPMENTS IN AMERICAN PHILOSOPHY
PART II

ETHICS, SOCIAL AND POLITICAL PHILOSOPHY

The practicality of American thought continues in the ideas of contemporary philosophers who work in moral, social, and political philosophy on individualism and community, American feminist ethics, and African American philosophy. Representing the last six decades of American philosophy, the philosophers discussed in this chapter share concerns about and offer solutions to problems of social justice and political ideals. Their ideas range from **libertarian** to communitarian, from assimilationist to separatist, and from philosophies of justice to philosophies of love.

THE INDIVIDUAL AND THE COMMUNITY

John Rawls (1921–2002) renewed interest in social contract theory in the 1950s with his article "Justice as Fairness" (1957) and in his groundbreaking 1971 book, *A Theory of Justice*. His version of contract theory is a Kantian expression of liberal democratic society founded on the rights of individuals.

In Rawls' contractarianism, Kant's ethical theory takes pride of place. Rawls rejected utilitarianism because its focus on the greatest happiness leads to the use of some people for the benefit of a majority.

He rejected **intuitionism** because it is impossible to reach agreement on intuited principles. Where utilitarianism and intuitionism fail to secure rights and dignity, applying Kantian ethics to the basic structure of society solves the problem of how to arrange society for the promotion of the common good.

To understand justice is to understand fairness. Rawls contended that it is not unfair that people occupy different positions in society or that there are disparities in distribution of wealth. Unfairness exists when people who occupy privileged positions got there at least in part through the disadvantages of others. Rawls did not seek to remove social differences, but to regulate them.

Rawls' theory is regulative in deriving principles from a fair procedure to ensure justice. The principles of justice for the proper organization of society are patterned principles derived as a matter of **pure procedural justice**. To achieve a fair, unbiased condition from which principles of justice may be formulated, Rawls proposes a hypothetical thought experiment reminiscent of the traditional contract theorists' state of nature. Rawls calls it the "**original position**." The original position is the position from which original contractors will, in employing reason, derive principles of justice for the right ordering of society. It is important to note that Rawls' goal is not to start over from scratch through literal political revolution, but to derive principles of justice that can be applied to existing societies.

The original contractors in the hypothetical original position deliberate with each other about potential principles of justice under the "**veil of ignorance**." They deliberate about what principles would be accepted if no one knew particular and contingent facts about their own lives and circumstances such as age, race, economic status, physical or other disability, and so on. The goal is to remove bias. What remains to the contractors is that they know they all require **primary goods** and that they all seek the good.

That they are all different individuals means that they may all have a different conception of the good life. Primary goods are what people will want regardless of whatever else they want. Rawls' procedure allows diverse people to strive for diverse goals, where all goals depend on the satisfaction of basic wants and needs. The procedure takes into consideration that self-interested people wish to find themselves in the best possible social position given their own particular, contingent, and specific circumstances once the "veil of ignorance" is lifted.

What it means to be in the best possible social position is that even if one finds himself in less than ideal circumstances in actual life, the principles of justice will achieve the goal of maximizing the minimum position with a **maximin strategy**. No one wishes to be at the bottom of the range of social positions in any society, and it is not fair or just to make their position worse when it could be made better. If an original contractor does not know whether he is Christian or Muslim, if he does not know whether he is rich or poor, and if he does not know any other contingent characteristics about himself during the decision procedure to create principles of justice, upon lifting the "veil," no person will be in a position in which he is disadvantaged because of such contingencies. **Rationally self-interested** people want the best they can obtain for themselves to have a chance to live out reasonable life plans.

Justice is found in fair procedures arising from a rational starting point with a slate nearly as clean as the Cartesian mind after engaging in hyperbolic doubt. From the original position under the veil of ignorance, rationally self-interested people will derive two principles of justice that are **categorical imperative**s. A categorical imperative, derived from reason, is universally applicable, ensures respect for persons, and recognizes that each person is an autonomous and rational moral agent capable of giving rules to himself.

The principles of justice are rules without exceptions because they are categorical imperatives. To be consistent with respect for persons, any rule derived must be such that it never allows any rational being to be treated as a means to an end. Rawls concluded that there are two principles of justice arising from the original position. They are **"The Equal Liberty Principle"** and **"The Difference Principle."** The equal liberty principle is that each person is to have an equal right to basic liberties that are compatible with the liberties of others. Equal liberties include voting rights, freedom of assembly, and others that are essential to participation in a democratic society. The difference principle is that social or economic inequalities must be arranged so that they are to everyone's advantage and be connected to positions that anyone may occupy.

The equal liberty principle takes priority over the difference principle. The difference principle is designed to support the equal liberty principle so that when there are disparities in wealth, status, or opportunities, any such disparities are consistent with equal liberty. Another way to put the case is that the equal liberty principle constrains the difference principle so that the only reason to limit liberty is to obtain more liberty. In essence, it is never in anyone's interest to be oppressed, and the equal liberty principle is a safeguard against oppression. No rational person would give up liberty for economic security, for example, because in giving up liberty, one may give up the right to enjoy economic security – in which case both of the principles of justice are violated.

Rawls' theory leads to a welfare state in which inequalities in wealth and opportunity are corrected by redistribution of wealth and property to ensure that the conditions of the equal liberty principle are satisfied. It is important to remember that for Rawls, the original contractors agree to the difference principle, an egalitarian principle of redress and reciprocity. The underlying concept is that no person would want to be better off if it meant that others would be worse off. The difference principle requires that when some people occupy more lucrative positions, it may be necessary for them to accept redistribution of some portion of their economic goods (through taxes, for example) so that the free exercise of the liberties of others may be realized and protected.

It is to Rawls' principles of justice as patterned and redistributional that Robert Nozick (1938–2002), a contemporary and colleague of Rawls, takes significant exception. Nozick's position on the nature of the distributive principle of justice is significantly different from that of Rawls in important ways, but both agree that it is individuals and their rights that are of primary importance.

Nozick, a libertarian contractarian, uses both Kantian and Lockean principles to formulate a theory of distributive justice. His acceptance of the Kantian respect for human dignity and the Lockean view of property inform Nozick's theory of justice from *Anarchy, State, and Utopia* (1974).

Kant held that every person has inherent dignity and must not be treated in any way contrary to that ideal. Locke argued that every person has a right to property and the right to do with his property as he sees fit just so long as he does not violate the rights of others. Nozick contended that based on these considerations, Rawls' theory is neither just nor fair.

Nozick's position is that Rawlsian principles of justice are patterned principles, set up in advance of actual historical conditions of ownership of property. He explained that Rawls' principles are inconsistent with human motivation because they require that people are sometimes deprived of some portion of their wealth or possessions they have obtained as a result of fair conditions of acquisition.

Fair conditions of acquisition are described in Nozick's historical principles of justice. The **principle of justice in acquisition** and **the principle of justice in transfer** are "historical" principles, which means that having rights to things depends on the origin of holdings. Nozick's principles are very simple. The principle of justice in acquisition is that a person is entitled to property when he has acquired it in a way that does not violate the rights of others. That is, for example, that he did not steal from others. The principle of justice in transfer is an extension of the principle of justice in acquisition in that a person who has received property from another, and where the first has acquired property either through fair acquisition or prior transfer, has a right or is entitled to the thing transferred. Another way to put it is that just so long as a person acquires property without violating the rights of others (that is, without violating either of Nozick's principles), the holder of the property is entitled to it.

These principles are distinctly different from Rawls' difference principle, which Nozick calls "end state." **"End state" principles** are determined by how distribution *turns out* rather than how distribution *came about*. In Nozick's view, Rawls' difference principle respects neither persons nor their property and is therefore unjust. An end-state, patterned principle of justice like the Rawlsian difference principle is based on the supposition that things exist in the world that are both divisible and separable from people who possess them. To see why Nozick thinks Rawls' position is unjustified, consider a case like that which Nozick used to illustrate the meaning, importance, and *justice* of the principle of justice in holdings and the principle of justice in transfer.

Suppose there is a famous basketball player that many fans go to games to see. Suppose further that the fans are so impressed by the basketball player that in addition to the ticket price, they also drop an extra $1.00 in a box labeled with the famous player's name and all the extra dollars go only to that single player. He will then receive both his regular salary as a member of the team and an extra amount equal to the number of dollars deposited into the box. The question is whether the player is entitled to the extra money. Nozick's answer is that he certainly is entitled to it. The reason he is entitled to it is explained by understanding the relationship between Nozick's principles of justice.

Assume for the sake of simplicity that the fans acquired the money they put in the box in a fair process of acquisition (e.g., they worked for it or it was given to them by someone who had a right to it). The money they put in the box is theirs until the moment they put it in the box, at which time they have transferred the right to the money to the basketball player. If the people who put the extra dollars in the box had a right to do with those dollars as they saw fit because they obtained the money under fair conditions, then when the basketball player obtains extra funds from the fans, he has acquired a right to the money on the basis of the principle of justice in transfer.

But what about the other players? Do they have a right to the money in the box labeled with another player's name and intended only for him? Nozick's answer to this question is a simple and straightforward "No." One of the foundational elements of social existence, for Nozick, is liberty. Nozick's use of the Lockean conception of basic rights possession (liberty) is expressly given in the Lockean law of nature. It is the *liberty* that each person has to do with his property as he sees fit. Since a liberty is a right, the basketball player has a right to the extra money given to him by his fans.

One might object that there is a sense in which other players have a right to a portion of the excess proceeds in the box because without other members of the team, the famous player would not be in a position to receive extra money in the first place. Nozick rejects this claim, however, by arguing that we are not required to pay for benefits we receive from society simply because they are received. In the example of the basketball players, "society" is the team. Being a team member, however, does not justify the team sacrificing any individual for the benefit of other team members. It is surely true that the famous basketball player receives benefit overall from being a member of the team, but under ordinary circumstances the team members do not feel (or at least they should not feel) entitled to the salaries of other players. Each player has his own salary and some salaries may be different based on experience, expertise, or other characteristics of individual players. For further clarification, Nozick used an example of one person giving another person a book, but the recipient has not asked for it and did not agree to pay for it. If the recipient did not ask for the book and did not agree to pay for it, it is unjust for the original owner of the book to demand or extract payment from the recipient. This is just as wrong when groups do it. It is wrong to expect to be paid for a benefit provided to someone that the recipient did not agree or ask to receive. It is especially wrong when the group charges for the benefit but the group did not provide it, which is the case with the money given to the famous player by fans. It cost other players nothing for the famous player to receive additional money. The fans obviously do not charge the player to receive the extra funds – they give them to him. Why should the *other players* expect a return on that which was not theirs from the outset?

The case is the same for a state. If it is wrong for individuals to violate the rights of other individuals, it is wrong for the state to violate the rights of individuals. Since the state is formed by individuals for their benefit and to protect their rights, it makes no sense to believe that individuals would agree to a system in which their rights are systematically violated. The state is required to be neutral with respect to persons, but a system in which the legitimate holdings of an individual are taken from him for the benefit of others violates both neutrality and respect. It is individuals whose goods are taken, and what is taken are not unencumbered pieces of abstract property that come into the world unattached to persons. Nozick contended that all holdings belong to someone, that they come into the world attached to individual persons or to groups who have sole and exclusive rights to them. A system like that of Rawls does not recognize ownership in this way and requires that a person (the basketball player) make sacrifices (give up the extra money, or some portion of it) to others. To require this of him on the basis of the difference principle is, in Nozick's view, to violate the player's rights. The individual player has a right to the money, and he has a right to determine what will be done with it (to keep it, give it away, or share it with other players). The point is that it is the famous player's right to choose how or whether to distribute his own property.

Nozick's individual rights-bearer therefore upsets Rawlsian patterned principles of justice because a right to the property on the Lockean view is inconsistent with the Rawlsian difference principle. For Nozick, end-state, patterned principles of justice are constantly interfering with individual lives and this is a clear, plain, and simple violation of the right that each person has *to be left alone* – that is, he has a right against others not to interfere in his liberty to dispose of his possessions as he sees fit. No individual, and no state, has a right to interfere in this right.

Unlike Rawls, then, Nozick argues for a minimal state. A **minimal state** (**minarchy**) is designed to protect citizens from violence, fraud, theft, and other violations of their persons and property and otherwise leaves people free to do as they wish in free and fair transactions. This conception of the limited power of the state, given content through Nozick's principles of justice, is a **night watchman state** and nothing more.

Michael Sandel (1953–), a contemporary and Harvard colleague of both Rawls and Nozick, argues that individual rights-based conceptions of the nature of morality and of the state are insufficient. Individualist theories of rights with attendant minimalist conceptions of our obligations to each other and no overriding conception of the good exemplify what Sandel considers a serious problem. The problem is that they have no sufficient (or any) moral foundation.

In his 1984 essay, "The Procedural Republic and the Unencumbered Self" and his more recent books such as *Democracy's Discontent* (1998) and *Public Philosophy* (2006), Nozick argues that without a moral foundation, it is impossible to formulate a complete political theory. Another way to put the case is that in liberal theories such as those of Rawls and Nozick, there is insufficient attention paid to actual and lived social and political arrangements of real human beings.

The political liberalism of Rawls and Nozick does not require a common conception of the good, so political liberalism depends on abstract rules and procedures with no reference to clearly defined goals. Without a common goal, there really is no community at all. If a fully functioning democratic society depends on the articulation and acceptance of a common goal between citizens to frame and form their actions, duties, obligations, and rights, rights-possessing *isolated* individuals cannot participate fully in the community. In fairness to Rawls and Nozick, they made it clear that they did not intend their theories of the structure and organization of political societies to be used to formulate complete ethical theories. Nonetheless, Sandel contends that the unencumbered, isolated individuals of political liberalism who choose their own conceptions of the good are the reason for "democracy's discontent."

Democracy's discontent comes about as the result of two significant fears facing contemporary liberal societies. They are the fear that people have lost self-government and that our communities are coming apart because they have no moral center. As **unencumbered selves** people have no say and no responsibility for choosing the ends of the group or government of which they are a part. In the liberal individualistic view of Rawls and Nozick or in any society formed on the basis of a procedural conception of justice, people have no sense of belonging to a group, they have no goals in common with others, and they have no secure bond with others. Each person is assumed to be sovereign over himself and has need for community only in the most minimal sense.

For Nozick, people are not and should not be as the liberal individualist conceives of them. We instead come into the world as members of families, we grow in societies in which a culture helps to determine who we are, and from the start we are encumbered selves. To think we are not is to think of ourselves as abstractions (like the individuals in Rawls' original position who know nothing except that they have interests and needs) and not as human beings.

For Sandel, the interests of individual human beings are bound up with the societies in which they live. We are members of communities such as families, nations, neighborhoods, and so on. If this is true, and if conceiving of oneself as an active, participating member of a community is essential to living a good life, then Rawls' and Nozick's political ideals are incomplete.

To think of ourselves as unencumbered, rationally self-interested and isolated individuals out only to protect our rights and to seek individual conceptions of the good fails to capture the fact of our relational nature. That is, we come into the world embedded in communities having ties, relationships, and obligations to others that in part define who we are. The problem of liberal societies putting forth liberal public philosophies, then, is that in the march toward liberty characterizing Rawls' and Nozick's theories, there is no inspiration, there are no goals, there is no sense of community, and no sense of civic engagement in which freedom can be used.

If we are indeed social beings (as Aristotle and Sandel and many others claim we are), the liberal individualist conception of the person is paltry and incomplete at best. Individuals are capable of morality but have no theory or framework to which to look for guidance. For the communitarian virtue-theorist we are not abstract individuals required to respect each other's rights simply by not interfering with them. We are members of communities in which a sense of belonging and concern for others are natural and real. With pure procedural systems of justice like those of Rawls and Nozick, we become writers of moral, social, and political plays, but no actors occupy meaningful roles.

The solution to the problem of the anomie, isolation, and self-lessness created by a society in which our selves, our rights, and our communities and government are no more than abstractions with rules, is to try to regain the sense of purpose and connectedness that is natural to human beings. But simply recognizing our existence as relational beings is not the solution. Sandel argues that there are problems of corruption in the republican tradition of encumbered selves, not least of which are the danger of "group-think" and isolation as well as difficulties in being able to navigate the many community memberships that one may have. How is the encumbered person to know which moral, social, and political commitments are best to have? Sandel is convinced that such pro-blems are inevitable and that the only hope we have is that there will be someone, somewhere, who can make sense of it all and create or repair the civic life that we have lost, and on which democracy depends.

AMERICAN FEMINIST ETHICS: INDIVIDUALS, COMMUNITIES, AND POWER

The range of American feminist ethics is wide. Feminist theory is even wider, encompassing epistemology, metaphysics, political theory, and so on. Our focus is limited to American feminist ethics, and specifically to Carol Gilligan's groundbreaking work on stages of moral development, the ethics of care (primarily from the work of Virginia Held), and Marilyn Frye's analysis of the insidious and continuing problems of oppression and control of women.

Like most American philosophers, American feminist ethicists tend to focus on applying arguments to solve real-life problems. For American women no less than for the revolutionaries, the Transcendentalists, the Pragmatists, and Native and African American philosophers, the point is to change things for the better. To do so requires careful consideration and analysis of theory and action to effect needed changes. Work on theories of moral development, a fully stated feminist ethics of care, and consideration of aspects of domination and inequality will show ways in which the voices of American women make and demand changes in traditional conceptions of morality, social and political life, and how to do this from actual, lived experience.

Even though Carol Gilligan (1936–) is not a philosopher, her groundbreaking work on ethics, *In A Different Voice* (1982), changed conceptions of the applicability and accuracy of traditional ethical theories. Gilligan noticed when working with Lawrence Kohlberg, a psychologist studying stages of moral development, that the responses of girls and boys to moral dilemmas were different in content. Kohlberg set up a classification system for moral development indicating that the highest levels of moral reasoning are reached when a person responds to moral dilemmas taking a "justice" approach. This approach privileges rational and individualistic responses on the model of social contract theory and Kantian ethics. Boys tended to score "higher" than girls because boys' answers tended toward solutions to moral dilemmas concentrating on concern with rights and justice and the traditional view that our obligations are primarily to avoid violating the rights of others. Girls, on the other hand, tended to answer questions regarding moral dilemmas that ended with their placement on the scale of moral development much lower than that of boys because they did not speak of rights so much as highlighting the importance of relationships and the value of talking to others to try to find compromises or creative solutions to problems.

Gilligan doubted that boys employ more fully developed moral reasoning than girls. She designed her own study and found that girls' approaches to moral dilemmas and how to solve them tend to be "relational" rather than "rational" and "other-oriented" rather than individualistic. That these approaches are different does not indicate that one is "higher" or a more nuanced type of moral reasoning. Instead, the distinction between relational/rational and other/individual oriented theories shows that a more complete moral view requires taking both the ethics of care and the ethics of justice into consideration. Sympathy, compassion, and other supposedly "emotional" reasons for action that have been traditionally neglected because they are considered irrational are actually part of a more rich and complete conception of ethics than traditional moral theories.

Rather than to think that a rights- and justice-based form of moral reasoning is superior to that of care, Gilligan's research indicated that Kohlberg's scale of moral development is a skewed view of what counts as moral maturity or moral progress. Gilligan argued that an impersonal, "rational" view of moral maturity comes about through a socialization and learning process just as a personal, "relational" view does. Women's moral experience is centrally connected to relationships and caring rather than being developed or conceived on the model of abstract notions of justice and fairness. In short, an ethics of care embodying relationships and interrelatedness of human beings connected in familial or emotional ways highlights a fact that is ignored in the **ethics of justice**: that we are all interdependent beings. Gilligan's psychological research is therefore important to the feminist ethics of care.

Virginia Held is one of the primary expositors of the ethics of care. In various articles and in *The Ethics of Care* (2006), Held explains the basis and many of the implications of this moral theory. One of the most important points made by the care ethicist is that traditional moral theories are insufficient because they fail to recognize that human beings are relational beings. We all come into the world with a need to be cared for by someone and this for a very significant period of time. We are not abstract individuals. We are particular persons nurtured in caring relationships.

It will not do to say that the solution to the problem of traditional ethical theories failing to take women's experience into account is simply to bring women into their content. Adding women to the traditional theories would not solve the problem inherent in the ethics of justice: the omission of the emotional and the relational. What is needed is a "transformation" of moral theories so that they include experiences with care as *moral* experiences. Probably the main reason that traditional theories do not take experience of care as moral experiences is the traditional theories' concentration on the dichotomy between reason and emotion and the public and private spheres.

In the Western tradition, emotion is considered irrational, personal, and incapable of leading to universal claims about moral theory or practice. Reason, on the other hand, is exalted as the source of moral truth. If, however, "care" is a more robust and complete conception of morality, a transformation of traditional moral theories is required. The transformation begins by rejecting three main points of focus in traditional ethical theories: the distinction between reason and emotion, the distinction between public and private realms of experience, and the concept of a self.

In the history of Western ethics, emotion is considered less valuable than reason and is therefore insufficient as a source of ethical truth. Plato, Aristotle, Kant, and many others too numerous to mention, all made their disdain for emotion clear. Plato, for example, relegated emotion to the lowest level of the soul where "desire" resides; Kant claimed there was no place for emotion in ethics at all because variable emotions and desires would create hypothetical rather than categorical imperatives and thus lack universality.

Contrary to most traditional ethical views, far from it being the case that emotions and caring relations muddy the waters of ethics, caring relations clarify ethical practice and give it a truly human orientation. Mothering, friendships, neighborhood associations, and other personal and particular human relationships highlight the private realm of real, lived, moral experience that does not appear in traditional ethical theories. Traditional theories discount the private realm and exalt that of the public. The private realm is that in which the "experience of women" is assumed to take place. It is the place in which children are cared for, meals are prepared, laundry is done, and in which biological functions and physical activities in the world of "mere" experience occur. Alternately, the public sphere is the "manly" realm in which warriors conquer other lands, heroes are honored for bravery, and business and political leaders work their will in making products, money, and important decisions. The public sphere is supposed to be a very cerebral, rational, non-embodied realm (it really is not, if we just think about it a bit more) that is fit for the *man* of reason. The point, at least in part, is that the masculine realm of power, hierarchy, decision-making, and productivity is generally held in higher esteem than the lowly realm of dependency, following rules, and consumption of products in the private realm.

For the ethics of care, dividing the public and private and rational and relational realms of human existence is not necessary. Caring relationships are as much part of what it is to shape and be a human being as the public realm, and in fact it may be more central because the private realm is where moral *human* beings are created. To deny "private" experience a place in the moral experience of all human beings is to have a truncated and insufficient concept of what it is to be human. It is to think of people as competitors and conquerors in business and war, in academic settings, and other forms of intellectual labor, rather than seeing them also as cooperators and members of complex social relationships not all of which are hierarchical and dominating.

An ethics of care is not intended to replace traditional ethics of justice. There are conditions in which treating people on the model of justice is appropriate and there are those in which care is appropriate. It is appropriate, for example, for a teacher to treat children in a classroom fairly and not show a preference for one over others (justice). On the other hand, there are other conditions in which care should override claims to simple justice, such as those in which treating everyone equally does not literally mean that they receive "equal shares" of goods, attention, or benefit in exactly the same way (to think of "equality" this way is an "impartial justice" view). A simple example is sufficient to make the point. It makes no sense to insist that men and women be treated equally in undergoing prostate exams and Pap smears. Women have no need of the former and men no need of the latter. The point is that caring for others, and hence doing justice with respect to them, is more (and less) than treating them in exactly the same way as fully rational beings living in a public sphere. Not recognizing the differences between and benefits of the ethics of justice and the ethics of care impoverishes moral theory and practice.

Marilyn Frye (1941–), a radical lesbian separatist feminist who focuses attention on difference to combat oppressive practices that are deeply engrained in moral, social, and political contexts, has important points to make regarding the continued oppression of women. Her view is not an ethics of care, but neither is it an ethics of justice. It is thoroughly separatist.

As women have unfortunately found, it will not do to try to solve problems of oppression and discrimination simply by ignoring differences such as race and gender and concentrating on "our essential humanity" in the hope that problems will dissolve. Early liberal feminists realized through first-hand experience that arguing that all humans are rational and should have the right to vote did not solve all their problems. Insidious forms of oppression and control continue to be wielded over women and the revolution in thought and action to end women's subordination is still incomplete.

Marilyn Frye's analysis of oppression and enslavement and its continuation in vicious and devious ways is part of revolutionary action in knowing how to resist and eliminate them. Frye does not argue that men and women are "the same." She doubts that they are and that there will ever be complete equalization. She is, then, a separatist. Her goal is to free women from patriarchy by creating a vision of what it would be like for all human beings, and especially women, to live without the "**arrogant eye**."

Frye explains her position with powerful imagery and examples nearly all women can understand. That nearly all women understand but that most men do not is part of the power of Frye's argument. She contends that women become much like slaves in patriarchal societies and are inadvertently complicit in it. To understand Frye's point, consider Edwards' or Locke's explanation of "freedom." For them, to be free is to be unhindered in doing what one wishes to do such that even a person locked in a room is "free" when he does not wish to leave since he is doing what he wants to do. In this view, a person is constrained only when he wants to leave and cannot do so. Frye's reaction to this simple, popularly held, and incorrect view of the nature of freedom is that it depends on the dubious assumption that what a person wants to do is the result of his own free choice. It is easy to say that a woman living in abusive conditions is *free* to leave and *can* leave if she *wants* to leave and so she is not being coerced into staying. But the simplicity of the statement hides the fact that it rests on a distortion of the meaning of "coercion."

The view of Edwards and Locke makes it seem that a person can be coerced only when physically constrained. So if a woman is threatened with death by a rapist and she "consents" to his demands, she "freely" engaged in sexual activity with him and proof positive of it is that she did not fight him or try to run away. In reality, she had no more freedom in the matter than the person with a gun to his head is free not to give the thief with the gun his wallet. Certainly, both the woman and the robbery victim are "free" to say no, but what this means is that they are free to be killed, which is certainly not "freedom" under any reasonable interpretation of the term.

Subtle forms of control in patriarchal society take place. A dominating male will manipulate a woman into losing a sense of self-respect and concern for herself and instead she sees her entire being made to serve his interests. She has succumbed to the "arrogant eye."

A person possessed of the arrogant eye believes that the world and everything in it in some way exists for him. People who believe that the Earth was created for the use and enjoyment of man, for example, are "arrogant perceivers." Arrogant perceivers believe the world belongs to them and this is the way it is meant to be. The arrogant perceiver wants to dominate nature, he wants to dominate things (men regularly refer to the machines they "get into" and that they "drive" as "she"), and they want to dominate women. Because most men are arrogant perceivers, they believe that the world was designed for them and what they do is right.

Women may also come to believe that the world exists for them, that they also have the capacity to dominate. It is unfortunate, Frye notes, that women can and do become arrogant perceivers. They do this when they see through the arrogant eye with a strange, perverted perception of the world in which they believe that they should be selfless and live for others. When the selfless person lives for others, it is doubtful that she actually loves those for whom she sacrifices.

What Frye hopes we will achieve to overcome patriarchy is to replace the "arrogant eye" with the "**loving eye**." With the loving eye, we recognize others as independent beings with value and dignity who are never rightly dependent or enslaved. We will form communities of difference and respect in our relationships with each other. Frye notes, however, that we have never achieved the loving eye and we will have to wait to see what happens when and if we do.

Carol Gilligan has shown how traditional ethical theories fail to take into account different moral "voices" of men and women. Virginia Held argued that an ethics of care is a viable alternative or addition to traditional theories in that it takes into account our relatedness and lived experience. Marilyn Frye shows that even if we succeed in making great strides in achieving opportunities and recognition for women, patriarchal societies are steeped in practices of oppression that are not solved merely by tendencies toward equality of men and women or creating new or altering old ethical theories. Lived experience and careful recognition of one's own oppressive behaviors are a start in truly respecting the dignity and value of every human being.

AFRICAN AMERICAN SOCIAL THOUGHT

Like much of the history of American philosophy, African American thought centers on concerns with equality, rights, and justice. It is not that African Americans are not interested in or have not excelled in other areas of philosophy. It is simply that as a distinctive movement, African American philosophy arises from struggle against inequality, oppression, unfairness, discrimination, fear of death, despair, and hopelessness in a society that has consistently failed to treat them with dignity, respect, and concern. In what follows, I hope to provide sufficient range of content in African American thought to express at least part of its distinctiveness and importance and to highlight it as representing what I believe is best in all of American philosophy. To achieve that end, we consider the philosophy of love of Martin Luther King, Jr., the black feminist ethics of bell hooks, and the "**Prophetic Pragmatism**" of Cornel West.

King (1929–68) was an assimilationist who sought racial unity through a philosophy of love by freeing people on both sides (racists and the oppressed) from the bonds of oppression. Oppression of African Americans comes about as a result of social convention and unjust laws. Jim Crow laws enacted in the American South after the Civil War were expressions of vitriolic white hatred of African Americans. To confront and to act against unjust laws was, for King, a duty above social conventions. It was a duty to live by one's convictions, to realize freedom through autonomous action, and to affirm the dignity of the human being.

Acting against unjust laws is a duty in the tradition of Socrates and Thoreau. Socrates refused to stop being a "gadfly" to fulfill his duty to question everything and seek wisdom. Refusal to compromise led to his death. Thoreau went (briefly) to jail for refusing to pay taxes to a government whose policies and actions he considered immoral. Socrates exemplifies the high moral calling to live according to one's convictions and Thoreau exemplifies the duty to **civil disobedience** and to **non-violent protest** against injustice. King adopted and lived by these duties.

King's goal to realize a society of fairness was a calling and commitment to justice. In *Letter from the Birmingham Jail* (1963), King pointed out that segregation laws were unjust because they were contrary to human dignity and put in place to benefit the majority at the expense of the minority. It was his duty to violate unjust laws. There is no immorality in violating unjust laws and in fact it is the *right* thing to do. Unjust laws like segregation damage human beings, and not only those at whom discrimination is directed. Damage to human beings comes about as a result of the segregated person coming to feel inferior to the segregator, and the segregator gaining a false sense of superiority in being a dominator.

King's philosophy of love requires civil disobedience to do what is right and just and to change unjust laws and the people who support them. King's philosophy of love is intended to be transformative for both the African American and for the white racist segregationist. The racist who feels superior to the African American is redeemed by love; so is the oppressed person who believes that he is nobody and nothing. Both of them need and receive redemption from King's way of love and non-violence.

It is reasonable to wonder how non-violent resistance will work. Why would an oppressor be moved by non-violent protest? King's position is that non-violent resistance exposes the weaknesses of the racist, it lowers the morale of the oppressor, and it awakens his conscience. Racists who attacked non-violent protestors made their character weaknesses manifest. Physically attacking those who are not threatening anyone is an expression of fear. The view that the African American is moved only by passion and not by intelligence or conviction is dispelled in the clash between the irrational behavior of whites who kick and arrest non-violent protestors and the calm and peaceful behavior of the protestors who will not satisfy the desires for violence of their white oppressors. Further, the oppressor who feeds his feelings of superiority by the ability to dominate African Americans finds himself unable to continue the charade. The oppressor is irrational, not the protestor. If the process of non-violence works, the white oppressor should come to feel guilt or shame in having behaved so badly, irrationally, and unjustifiably.

Even more important, however, is that the African American, through non-violent resistance in a philosophy of love, develops self-respect, courage, and dignity that were lost in oppressive conditions. The African American can come to see that in solidarity with others he has the capacity to change the way things are. Taking a stand against unfairness, being able to show why it is wrong, reinforces in the person a sense of his value and dignity. In essence, as King noted, the point is not to defeat and humiliate the opponent (the oppressor), but to turn him into a friend and gain his understanding. King's non-violent philosophy of love is a start, but there is much more to do.

Bell hooks (1952–) writes in a wide variety of areas in feminist theory and African American philosophy, but it is one particular aspect of her work to which we turn our attention. Hooks notes in *Feminist Theory: From Margin to Center* (1984) that feminism in the 1800s and feminism in the 1960s were not that different in one striking way: in both, the concerns of black women were ignored. While Betty Friedan made significant waves with *The Feminine Mystique* (1963), she ignored non-white women and poor women in writing from the point of view of a bored white housewife who wanted more out of her life than taking care of children and staying home to do it. As hooks makes clear, there are women who have no home in which to take care of children and who do not have the choice not to work outside the home if they have one. Their experience is not represented by the white woman feminist. Hooks' point is that early feminism expressed the same kind of universalist and all-encompassing attitude expressed by the ancients, the moderns, the Church, and all other groups and institutions for which being dominant caused them to suffer blindness to their own prejudices and unwarranted assumptions – or not to care that they had them at all.

What distinguishes a woman like Betty Friedan from many other women whose lives have been omitted from consideration in feminist ethics is that middle-class and wealthy white women did have choices, so they were not oppressed. They suffered discrimination and exploitation, but they had the ability to decide whether they would work outside the home or take care of their children, and they had the choice to take their children – if they worked outside the home – to day care. Like Frye, hooks recognizes that oppression is absence of choices, and rich and middle-class white women had choices. But in cases in which white women felt they were subject to discrimination and exploitation, they concentrated so heavily on the atomistic and individualistic account of human life that they ignored both the community and the conditions of those quite unlike themselves. White and black feminists were not able to find a point of connection.

By the peculiar position in which white women are placed (as oppressors of black women and men), and due to black male oppression of black women, black women are oppressed and exploited by other women *and* by men. Hooks' concern is to make this clear and to work toward liberation in theory and in practice.

Liberation is not found in achieving equality with white men. To be equal to men gives women an interest in oppressing others. A good example of women becoming oppressors is E. C. Stanton, who argued for women's equality with men while at the same time being appalled that black men were granted the right to vote while white women were not. For all of Stanton's good work in the early women's rights movement, her racist tendencies unfortunately sometimes overrode her good sense. Believing that equality with white men will set women free from oppression, exploitation, and discrimination is, therefore, simply wrong. It turns out that when women seek equality with white men, they deny unity and connection with other women, falling into lockstep with the tradition of male-dominated societies like ours and thinking in terms of individuals and their rights rather than thinking of the connections they have with others.

When people lack connection with each other, hooks argues, they cannot see themselves as sisters in a feminist revolution and they are then unable to break free from the oppressive and exploitative conditions from which they wish to escape. Hooks astutely observes what Emma Goldman had noted many years before – that gaining the right to vote was ineffective in making important and needed changes in American society. Hooks does not argue against women having a right to vote, but instead she notes that women tend to vote in ways that are contrary to their own interests in voting the way men in their families vote, and thus do not change their lot in life. Instead, they tended to help support the patriarchy of white racism that existed from the start. Feminism, therefore, in hooks' view, is not only about ending male domination and women having equal rights with men. It is, instead – and much like Frye's vision of a new life for women – a feminism in which all forms of domination are removed from society. Removing domination requires community action, and like Sandel, hooks realizes that community action requires people to recognize that they have connections to each other in important ways that can lead them to action to benefit themselves and American society – and indeed all racist, sexist, homophobic, classist, and oppressive societies – by setting their sights on the development of people.

Cornel West's (1953–) "prophetic pragmatism" combines the traditional African American sense of hope in the Church in fighting racism and pragmatic cultural criticism in search of a community of love and hope. While West does not proffer a philosophy of love on the model of Martin Luther King, Jr., he shares with King the conviction that to achieve goals of gaining respect for African Americans and improving their condition in American society it is best to take the path of cooperation rather than that of divisive separatist action. Where King would not align himself with the violence of **Black Nationalism** or the hopelessness of African Americans who had unfortunately bought into American culture's picture of black as inferior, West says in *Race Matters* (1994) that there are two causes of degradation and lack of self-respect among African Americans. They are: black middle-class insistence upon assimilation with and approval of white Americans and the Black Nationalists' fixation on white racism. Neither of these approaches will have the desired effect to cure "despair, dread, disappointment, disease, and untimely death" that characterize African American life in the United States.

West believes that the job of the African American philosopher is to continue to work toward a revolutionary future that is better than the present and in which oppression of *all* people is eliminated or reduced in scope and effect. African American philosophers have always maintained the revolutionary goal to improve the future by alleviating or eliminating oppression, but early work in African American philosophy did not go far enough to achieve the goal. West's goal is to take the traditions of African American thought beyond the early stages into a critique of capitalist, racist society that continues to oppress African Americans.

The African American quest for self-respect and self-determination is, for West, facilitated and expressed by combining with Black Liberation Theology. Liberation Theology's message for African Americans at the outset was that slaves were like Jews enslaved by Egyptians. Slaves were possessed of the same kind of power and fortitude to allow them to become free. For West in *Prophesy Deliverance! An Afro-American Revolutionary Christianity* (1982) and in other works, Christianity and the African American community's attachment to religious practice are part of the ethics and politics of self-respect. Their reading of scripture is communal as well as individual; it is religious as well as secular.

The communal nature of prophetic pragmatism is to realize the need for social awareness to fight injustice. It is therefore applicable also to those who do not have and do not seek a "religious" affiliation but who wish to fight against injustice in their community. The value of the individual human being as well as of the community of oppressed and oppressor are brought together in West's work in a way similar to that of King in the notion that love allows people to affirm their humanity. Within community they can work toward recognition of full human status for all people. Accepting Christianity is not a requirement of West's view, but he seeks the high values of it in love and care for others and the centrality of community in which every person values every other.

Unfortunately, we live in a society in which it is often the case that market forces and material goods take precedence over the value of humanity. West seeks a society realizing that human dignity and value take precedence over all other social values and that the power of love, in a way reminiscent of King's manner of arguing for a philosophy of love directed toward change and the rectification of injustice, ensures that the weakest members of a society are not ignored, not further oppressed, and are by the influence of love in a community empowered, free, and valued.

West's view of the power of community to raise individuals to self-respect and to move communities to action to fight oppression seems closely associated with the feminist ethics of care applied to civil society. If this is so, it helps to address at least part of Sandel's concern that we need to reinvent or repair civic life and it addresses hooks' concern that communal and sustained action are impossible without a feeling of connectedness.

West realizes that it is unreasonable to expect people who are convinced that they lack worth to feel an urgent need to take action against their condition, so centering on African American distinctness and difference is important. Claiming that there is no difference between white and black, between male and female, between rich and poor, will get us nowhere in encouraging people to rise up against injustice, oppression, and exploitation that our society breeds. "Color blindness" and mindless assimilationism in radically individualistic, modernist theories of ethics, society, and the state do nothing to fight against continuing racial subordination. Just as being a woman creates distinct differences in life experiences, being black is an essential part of the identity of the individual African American. West does not argue that we ought all to adopt the same ends or goals, but that instead we should see ourselves as part of various communities tied up in one civic community.

CRITICISMS

Sandel and feminist theorists critically evaluate individualist ethical and political theories like those of Rawls and Nozick. There are standard difficulties with contract theories regarding whether people can agree in advance to principles applied outside the realm of actual experience and whether what a person *would agree* to in a condition of incomplete information about themselves *is applicable* in real political conditions.

It is possible that feminist ethicists are wrong in thinking that there are systemic problems in traditional ethical theories and that more careful and equitable application of them will alleviate problems generated by ignoring our relational selves. Care ethicists may also commit the very errors of which they accuse masculinist theorists in insisting in a universal fashion that everyone ought to adopt the ethics of care and be more compassionate and caring rather than more rational.

King and West may be too optimistic in thinking that an ethics of love will change the unrepentant racist. Communitarian and feminist theories of care are often criticized on the basis of the fear that putting the community and its interests before the rights of individuals may lead to the conditions of oppression and exploitation that feminists and African Americans try to eliminate. African American philosophers such as King, hooks, and West, however, may have found ways with a philosophy of love to overcome the difficulties of communitarian thinking and action in retaining difference to enrich communities.

CONCLUSION

West argues that social and political organization plagued by oppression, exploitation, unfairness, and injustice breaks down communities. The individual whose life has no meaning has no sense of the power of individuals in communities to make positive social changes. West's view is like King's lament that oppressed people feel powerless and some go so far as to believe that their lot in life is to be less valued and cared about because that is simply the way things are.

West's view also highlights Marilyn Frye's important distinction between the arrogant eye and the loving eye. The alarming condition of our society in which so many people feel their lives have no deep or real meaning, who have been brought up to believe that material success is identical to human value, and who feel no connection to each other in a shared human project, should wake up a slumbering America to realize that we are not as great as we think we are when many of our fellow citizens are hungry, poor, tired, homeless, oppressed, denied rights, and live in abject conditions from which our society, if it would live up to its ideals, could free them. West, Sandel, and Held all agree, and I agree with them, that a society giving all its attention to economic prosperity and thereby exploiting others is unjust. Injustice exists where individuals concentrate the bulk of their attention on self-interest and live on the model of the "rational man," the isolated, atomistic individual of modern moral and political thought who creates conditions in which there are no shared goals or ideals for people as members of communities. When people feel that they are not part of a group, that their interests need always to be protected *against* others, they do not see that they can help to sustain the rights and good of all through civic association formed by a Rortyan conviction that we are all in this life together.

Leonard Harris describes African American philosophy in the title of his book, *Philosophy Born of Struggle*. I think that the history of

American philosophy is rightly described this way as well. I have presented a history of American philosophy showing that it is largely characterized by revolutionary action, acceptance of the reality of change, and work toward social justice. The struggle of colonists against their oppressors, absolutists against fallibilists, men against women, Native Americans against their colonizers, African Americans against oppression, science and philosophy against ignorance and superstition, and oppression and unfairness against dignity and justice, are examples of the many ways in which American philosophy is born of and lives with struggle.

Americans have been struggling against injustices, and struggling for what is good, from the beginning of American society. Perhaps we can reach the laudable goals in Rorty's ironism and West's prophetic pragmatism. West develops a different kind of irony from that of Rorty in his tragicomic sense of hope and the ability of oppressed people to continue to find meaning in life despite despair. West's goal is like that of Rorty to see humanity's highest moral and social calling in developing solidarity with others to create the best lives for ourselves and others of which human beings are capable. If these are the results to which American philosophy is contributing, I am hopeful that American society will follow American philosophy's lead.

FURTHER READING

On individualism and community, see David Schmidtz, *Robert Nozick* (New York: Cambridge University Press, 2002); Norman Daniels, (ed.), *Reading Rawls: Critical Studies on Rawls' A Theory of Justice* (New York: Basic Books, 1975).

On feminist ethics, see Gerda Lerner, *The Creation of Patriarchy* (New York: Oxford University Press, 1986); Virginia Held, *The Ethics of Care: Personal, Political, and Global* (New York: Oxford University Press, 2006); and Marilyn Frye, *The Politics of Reality: Essays in Feminist Theory* (Freedom: Crossing Press, 1995). The *APA Newsletter on Feminism and Philosophy* has issues on elements of feminist ethics. See www.apaonline.org.

For African American philosophy, see Hanes Walton, Jr., *The Political Philosophy of Martin Luther King, Jr.* (New York: Greenwood, 1971); Leonard Harris, *Philosophy Born of Struggle: Anthology of*

Afro-American Philosophy from 1917 (Dubuque: Kendall/Hunt, 1983); John P. Pittman, (ed.), *African-American Perspectives and Philosophical Traditions* (New York: Routledge, 1997); Tommy Lott, *A Companion to African-American Philosophy* (Malden, MA: Blackwell, 2003); bell hooks' *Outlaw Culture* (New York: Routledge, 1994)

Maria del Guadalupe Davidson, (ed.), *Critical Perspectives on bell hooks* (New York: Routledge, 2009); George Yancy, (ed.) *Cornel West: A Critical Reader* (Malden, MA: Blackwell, 2001) and Rosemary Cowan, *Cornel West: The Politics of Redemption* (Malden, MA: Blackwell, 2003). The *APA Newsletter on the Black Experience* contains issues on hooks and West, among others, at www.apaonline.org.

GLOSSARY

abolitionism: ideological movement in the early nineteenth century to end slavery.

absolutism: belief system in ethical, social, epistemological, and metaphysical realms characterized by claims to certainty, fixity, and finality; associated with unchanging religious beliefs and totalitarian governments.

ad hoc: explanations provided to defend a position in an off-the-cuff manner without or with manufactured reasons.

Age of Reason: see *Enlightenment*.

alienation: in Marxist thought, the condition of human beings when humanity and human value are denied in capitalist societies.

Allegory of the Cave: in Plato's *Republic*, a story explaining the distinction between appearance and reality.

amphiarchate: shared rule of women and men; movement away from patriarchal forms of government.

analytic/synthetic distinction: traditional epistemological view that analytic and synthetic statements are of completely different kinds.

anarchism: a theory that all forms of government are unjustifiable and should be abolished because they are inconsistent with liberty; promotes a classless society.

anomaly: observation or event occurring during the practice of normal science that does not "fit" (i.e., that is inconsistent with) expected observations and results.

Anti-Federalism: a movement opposing the creation of a strong federal government. Compare *Federalism*.

antinomies/antinomy: pair of concepts which are contradictory but characterized by equally good arguments in their favor.

antinomies of pure reason: from Kant's metaphysics, pairs of incompatible concepts which cannot both be true but for which equally good reasons can be given.

a posteriori: knowledge or truths derived from experience.

a priori: knowledge or truths that are logically prior to experience.

a priori rationalism: Peirce's term for a method of fixing belief characterized by the notion that there are truths known immediately and with certainty without argument.

argument: any group of statements of which at least one is a conclusion (the point at issue) and one is a premise (a reason offered in support of the conclusion). Arguments are deductive (reach certainty), inductive (reach probability), or abductive (arguments to the best explanation).

arrogant eye: moral and social conviction among its possessors that the world and everything in it belongs to and is rightly controlled by and for their interests.

assimilationism: in feminist and African American philosophy, the belief that two or more disparate groups can find or create common ground among their disagreements and differences.

atheism: belief that there is no God.

authoritarianism: belief held by those who contend that the words of authorities or those in power are to be taken at face value without question or critical appraisal.

authority, method of: Peirce's term for closed social groups defending beliefs against alternate ideas.

autonomy: the characteristic of a being who is free and self-ruling.

benevolence: altruism; charity in relation to others.

Birthday Fallacy: error in reasoning in the Design Argument; claiming that everything has a cause means that everything has the same cause; compare to the notion that everyone has a birthday means everyone has the same birthday.

Black Liberation Theology: compares the plight of African Americans to that of Jesus, and that Christianity is a religion of the oppressed and poor.

Black Nationalism: African American radical separatism.

Calvinism(ists): fundamentalist Christianity holding with predestination and belief that human beings are irremediably sinful. People are saved by the unearned grace of God.

capitalism: economic theory in which workers sell their labor in competitive conditions; capitalists are the owners of the means of production (e.g., factories).

care, ethics of: see *ethics of care*

categorical imperative: the moral principle of deontological (Kantian) ethics requiring universality in application of moral rules and respect for persons.

chattels personal: movable property that includes anything animate or inanimate that is not "real" property (land).

Christianity: religion based on the teachings of Jesus (considered a divine savior) in the New Testament; promises salvation and eternal life and often considered a moral doctrine.

civil disobedience: acting against unjust laws in an attempt to change them and the social attitudes supporting them.

clarity and distinctness, criterion of (Descartes): result of hyperbolic doubt arising from the certainty that "I am; I exist" is true; in use, no statement is accepted as true unless it is necessarily (logically) true.

coherence theory of truth: belief that statements are true when the system of ideas in which they exist are consistent with each other.

"Color Line, The": boundaries put in place by white people (European-Americans) that divide and protect their economic and political interests from those of African Americans.

communitarianism: social view emphasizing the connection between the individual and the community. See *encumbered self*.

compatiblism: the position that human freedom and determination of the will are compatible with each other.

constitution: documentation of fundamental laws according to which a state is governed.

contradiction: a relationship between statements such that if one is true, the other must be false.

correspondence theory of truth: "common sense" position that ideas copy more or less the reality of things as they are.

Creation, accounts of: two Biblical stories of Creation, one in which Adam and Eve are created at the same time and one in which Eve is created after Adam.

Creationism/Creationist: theological belief in the literal account of Creation in the Old Testament.

Deism: rational religion; belief that there is a God, but neither personal nor involved in this world beyond the act of Creation.

demonstration/Demonstrative Knowledge: conclusions reached from intuitive truths in a process of reasoning. Demonstration has the same degree of certainty as intuitive truth.

deontology: Kant's ethics of duty requiring universal moral principles and respect for persons. Not concerned with consequences.

Design, Argument from/Design Argument: argument for God's existence relying on the notion that there are purposes and regularity in nature, leading to the claim that God is the intelligent designer of the universe.

determinism (hard): see also fatalism; the belief that every event in the universe has a cause and that the causal sequence of events cannot be changed.

Difference Principle: that disparities and wealth and opportunity are accounted for by being beneficial to all members of a society.

dilemma of determinism: in William James' pragmatism, the undesirable consequences resulting from belief in both a deterministic universe and judgments of regret regarding occurrences or events.

double consciousness: the perception of African Americans that their existence is split between being African and being American.

dualism: in metaphysics, that bodies and minds are both substances; generally, binary oppositional views such as good/bad, man/woman, heaven/Earth.

egoism: moral view that self-interest is either a characteristic of human nature or that it ought to be.

elect, the: in Calvinist theology, those destined for salvation.

Emancipation Proclamation (1863): presidential edict by Abraham Lincoln intended to end slavery.

embodied knowledge: "lived" knowledge in practices and habits related to one's physical existence and placement; non-rational.

empiricism: epistemological system in which ideas are derived only through sense experience.

encumbered self: conception of human beings as naturally parts of communities having essential relations to each other. See *unencumbered self.*

end-state principles: parts of a theory determining the results of an action, procedure, or policy.

Enlightenment: Age of Reason; characterized by reliance on reason in place of authority and tradition; recognizes the individual as autonomous.

enthusiasm, religious: see *religious enthusiasm.*

epistemology: theory of knowledge; concerned with nature, origins, limits, and reliability of knowledge.

epistemology, naturalized: see *naturalized epistemology*

Equal Liberty Principle: Rawls' principle that every person has a right to the most extensive system of freedoms available to all others.

ethics: philosophical study of the right and the good, the good life, and the nature, origin, and legitimacy of moral claims.

ethics of care: feminist theory recognizing human mutual-interdependence in moral theory and experience; contrary to "rights-based" ethics of justice focused on individual rights.

ethics of justice: general characterization of traditional Western moral theories that they are focused on abstract, rights-based principles concerned primarily with individual rights.

ethics, virtue: see *virtue-ethics.*

evil, moral: contrasted with natural evil (such as hurricanes, floods, and other natural disasters or occurrences leading to pain and suffering), moral evil is constituted by human actions; morally blameworthy actions caused by human beings such as murder, theft, lying, and dishonesty.

evil, problem of: epistemic difficulty involved in the clash between apparent evil in the world and the existence of an all-good God.

evolutionism: "extension" of the Darwinian theory of evolution in which adherents claim that the biological theory applies to social processes.

evolution, theory of: biological theory accounting for change and creation of species over time through mutations and adaptations to environment. Compare *Creationism.*

factions: a small or large group motivated by a common interest.

fallibilism: an attitude toward human knowledge acquisition and possession to avoid universalization and accept claims tentatively.

fatalism/fatalist: the view that we are powerless to do anything other than what we actually do; also that one's destiny is fixed.

Federalism: an arrangement of government in which powers are in an overriding federal system, and where all other rights are reserved to the states or principalities; support of strong central government.

feminism/feminist: a movement to define and establish equal or fair social, political, and economic rights for women.

feminist ethics: a variety of approaches to theoretical and applied ethics with emphasis on the inclusion of women's theorizing and women's practice in moral reasoning and practice.

freedom, Arminian radical: view regarding the will that it is affected by nothing; absolutely free. Associated with the Dutch theologian Jacobus Arminius.

geocentric theory: early scientific position that Earth is the center of the universe.

Great Awakening, American: movement in American Protestant Calvinism away from religious formalism and toward more personal and enthusiastic religious feeling and practice.

habit(s): common actions of individuals or groups used to solve problems.

heliocentric theory: scientific view that the Sun is the center of the universe.

human nature: an essence of humanity expressing a fundamental common point possessed by all.

hyperbolic doubt: Cartesian method of finding a firm foundation for knowledge through a process of doubting all things to reach certainty.

idealism: that all real things are immaterial rather than material. Associated with George Berkeley.

ideals: dreams and aspirations of people that are significant to the individual.

ideas, innate: conceptions that are inborn in the mind, in some cases said to be implanted by God. Contrasted with ideas received through sense experience.

incommensurability: inconsistency between theories or principles.

indeterminism: position regarding the will that there is "loose play" in the world rendering some actions or events as chance occurrences.

Inquisition, Spanish: Decree of Spanish monarchs, Ferdinand and Isabella, in the fifteenth century to maintain Christian Orthodoxy by ordering non-Christians to convert to Christianity or to leave the kingdom. The Inquisition was formally ended in the early nineteenth century.

Inquisitors: Representatives of the Church who suppressed any expression perceived as being at variance of that of the Church or a threat to Church/patriarchal authority.

instrumentalism: Deweyan notion that ideas are instruments to be used in solving problems.

intelligent design (ID): believed by Creationists; exists in opposition to the theory of evolution in denying mutation; belief in fixed species and teleology.

intuition: (or feeling) as understanding for Emerson; generally, reason or intuitive thought verifying the truth of a claim.

intuitionism: a position regarding knowledge that there are facts or truths known immediately without reasoning.

Jim Crow laws: discriminatory and unjust laws mandating racial segregation, leading to oppression of African Americans.

judgments of regret: one's opinion that whatever occurrence or action took place should have been otherwise.

Justified True Belief: definition of knowledge such that a statement is true, there are arguments in its favor, and a knower believes the statement is true.

knowledge, intuitive: intellectual comprehension of principles such as identity (that a thing is identical to itself), the principle of non-contradiction (that a thing cannot be both itself and not itself at the same time), and that "I exist," among others.

liberal irony: Rorty's politically liberal and hopeful stance regarding moral, social, and political conditions.

libertarian: with respect to the will, the view that it is not determined; with respect to political thought, the view that only limited government is justified to protect individuals from violations of their rights.

logic: The study of the methods and principles of correct reasoning.

logic, Aristotelian: specifically, the use of syllogistic reasoning; a general approach to reasoning in which the goal is to affirm conclusions through a stringent form of argumentation allowing no option for variable conclusions.

love, philosophy of: moral, social, and political view held by Martin Luther King, Jr. and bell hooks in which transformation of the person occurs through community membership and empowerment.

loving eye: a moral and social conviction that each person is an independent other and free from coercion and control.

martial virtues: traits of character such as strength, willingness to fight, and fortitude.

Marxism: philosophical and economic theory of Karl Marx. The view that workers should rule over society with the fall of capitalism; a moral view valuing humanity.

Marxism, anarchist: see *anarchism*.

master morality: Nietzschean term for the moral system of the Übermensch who creates his own values of strength and power.

materialism/materialist: metaphysical view that matter is a substance and therefore real.

matriarchate: moral, social, and political authority held by women. Compare *patriarchy*.

matters of fact: Hume's term for truths known by experience.

maximinstrategy: a position in social and political contexts derived from economic considerations indicating that the minimum social position or gain should be maximized for greatest gain.

metaphysics: inquiry into the nature of being, the character of reality.

method of authority: Peirce's characterization of a method of fixing belief depending on group cohesion to ensure purity of community's ideas to avoid outside influences and ideas.

method of science: Peirce's preferred method of inquiry in which belief is subject to test, verification, and falsification.

minimal state (minarchism): conception of the power and function of the state limited to protecting citizens from violations of persons or property such as theft, robbery, and rape; night watchman state; associated with Nozick's political theory.

monarch: political power vested in one ruler by divine or hereditary right.

moral evil: See *evil, moral.*

mutation: changes in natural things; primarily biological application.

naturalized epistemology: Quine's suggestion that theory of knowledge turn toward empirical observation and analysis of the character of human knowledge as psychological.

nature, state of: a hypothetical natural condition in which there is no government, no society, no social organization of any kind, in which people are in some way isolated from each other, having experienced little or no socialization.

negation of the negation: communism as the removal of capitalism and private property that negate humanity; restores human dignity and value.

"Negro Problem, The": W. E. B. Du Bois' term for the economic, social, and political position and condition of African Americans caused by social boundaries created by whites.

night watchman state: see *minimal state.*

non-violent protest/non-violent resistance: a social or political strategy of peaceful rather than violent civil disobedience to create social change.

normal science: the ordinary progress of science in experimentation, testing, and development.

noumena: Kantian term for things as they are. Compare *phenomena.*

omnibenevolence: characteristic of God as infinitely good.

omnipotence: characteristic of God as infinitely powerful.

omniscience: characteristic of God as all-knowing and infinitely wise.

option: alternative choices.

oral tradition: means of transmitting cultural knowledge and worldviews verbally rather than in written form, primarily in Native American and early African American philosophy.

original position: starting point in deriving principles of justice for the right ordering of society.

Over-Man: See *Übermensch.*

Over-Soul: Emersonian individual like Nietzsche's Übermensch; God-like.

paradigm: accepted theory of the rules, principles, and progress of science; scientific theory or worldview.

paradigm shift: occurs when one paradigm is replaced by another as a result of a scientific revolution.

Pascal's Wager: Blaise Pascal's argument that belief in God is more beneficial than non-belief and not attended by negative consequences.

patriarchy: moral, social, and political rule by men.

patterned principles of justice: an arrangement of society in which disparities in wealth and opportunity among the "most advantaged" members of society are accounted for by corresponding benefits to all its members.

pecuniary justice: the notion that the moral debt of one person can be paid by another person or being.

phenomena: Kantian term for the world of appearances. Compare *noumena*.

philosophy of science: an inquiry into the methods, principles, application, and meaning of science.

philosophy, political: inquiry into the nature, justification, extent, and power of governments or government systems.

philosophy, social: philosophical inquiry into the nature, justification, and meaning of freedom, rights, and justice.

positivism: way of conceiving of method in science related to the meanings of moral, scientific, and other terminology.

"Pragmatic Maxim": Peircean injunction in inquiry to ask ourselves what kind of practical effect ideas have.

Pragmatic Theory of Truth: that truth "becomes"; statements are made true by experience.

Pragmatism: a philosophical method; denies absolutes, fixity, and finality; concentrates on practical results in all realms of human inquiry and experience.

predestination: position that human beings are destined for salvation or for damnation, and that their destiny has been fixed through all eternity; rejects "good works" as a means of salvation.

primary goods: rights and objects necessary for survival and the ability to work toward one's own goals based on a conception of the good.

principle of justice in acquisition: a person has a right to property acquired when obtained without violating the rights of others.

principle of justice in transfer: a person has a right to property when it has been transferred from another who had a right to it by prior acquisition or transfer.

principle of nature's uniformity: the belief that the future will resemble the past.

principle of universal causation: see *universal causation, principle of.*

Prophetic Pragmatism: moral, religious, social, and political view of Cornel West combining Liberation Theology and pragmatic social criticism leading toward a more just society.

pure procedural justice: derivation of principles of justice through means that are themselves fair and unbiased.

Puritanism: group in Protestantism in the seventeenth century whose main doctrines are purity, piety, and "predestination"; only a few "elect" are chosen by God to be "saved."

racism: beliefs and behaviors arising from stereotypes regarding race and color, leading the racist to believe that members of another race are inferior. In practice, racist beliefs lead to behaviors and policies discriminating against people based on their racial heritage or identity.

rationalism/rationalist: doctrine that some ideas are innate; general view that the nature of true knowledge is certain.

rational self-interest: looking out for one's own welfare but without simplistic concentration on self-interest to the detriment of others.

"Reason" (Emerson): Feeling/intuition will lead to knowledge of what is ultimately real by transcending sense experience.

reconstruction in philosophy: Deweyan method applied to traditional philosophy to avoid absolutism, dualism, and unnecessary philosophical conundrums.

relations of ideas: Hume's term for necessary truths; truths of reason. Compare *matters of fact.*

religion, philosophy of: inquiry into the nature and existence of God; religious practices, rituals, and meaning; the nature of religious/ divine commands, the problem of evil, and associated problems.

religious enthusiasm: belief that religious truths are known through a divine light or sense of the heart in a non-rational and emotional way.

resolutive-compositive method: A method in which a problem (a complex thing) is broken down into its smallest possible components so that the internal workings of a whole can be understood by analysis of its parts.

rights, civil: for Paine, freedoms that are ineffective in the individual that must be protected by government. A sub-set of natural rights.

rights, natural: Universal, unalienable rights not dependent on laws of any government.

scientific revolution: occurs when normal science fails to account for anomalous occurrences and a new scientific theory replaces the current one.

self, encumbered: who a person is as defined by their society, and determined by social status, belief, ethnicity, and membership in that society.

self-sovereignty: position of Elizabeth Cady Stanton asserting the right and duty of each person to develop independence in thought and action through the development of human autonomy, strength, and education.

sense of the heart: a "sixth sense" in Jonathan Edwards' theology possessed by the elect that lets them know the true nature of God. See *elect, the*.

sensitive knowledge: For Locke, the third degree of knowledge without the certain character of intuition and demonstration and is therefore not truly knowledge.

separatism: social and political view that races and sexes should find social and political refuge in their own communities, trusting in their own ability and worth.

skepticism: attitude toward knowledge claims characterized by doubt about their veracity, reliability, and applicability.

slave morality: Nietzschean term for moral systems of dependency and weakness, especially in Judeo-Christian religion and society.

social contract theory: theory of government resting on the notion that a state or society exists by the agreement of individuals for their benefit.

solidarity: fellow-feeling, empathizing with the plight of others and oneself.

statement, analytic: necessarily true; subject and predicate are synonymous.

statement, synthetic: contingently true; predicate amplifies the concept of the subject.

Stoic/Stoicism: philosophical view that one should not be concerned with what cannot be changed; approaching the world and its problems with calm and peacefulness; accepting conditions.

suffrage: the right to vote in political contexts and to run for political office

surplus value: the difference between the cost to produce a product and sale of the product, resulting in profit.

Talented Tenth: the ten percent of African Americans in Du Bois' philosophy who will achieve academic and social prominence, proving African American abilities and worth.

teleology: end- or goal-based actions or theories.

teleological argument: argument for God's existence resting on the notion that there must be an intelligent designer of this universe which expresses rationality in Creation and in which all things exist for a purpose.

tenacity, method of: Peirce's term for individuals who protect their beliefs by isolating themselves from alternate ideas and opinions.

theodicy: belief that there is no evil in the world or if evil does exist, God creates or allows evil so that the result is the best of all possible worlds.

theory of perception, representative or causal: epistemological view that our perceptions or ideas are like copies or images of things as they actually are and that things as they are cause our perceptions of them.

three–fifths clause: element of the U.S. Constitution counting each African American slave as three-fifths of a person to determine congressional representation in states.

totalitarianism: character of political states with absolute power.

Transcendentalism/Transcendentalists, New England: American moral, social, and political movement in which unique individuals and a uniquely and distinctively American society are to be created through self-reliant individualism and striving for human greatness.

transvaluation of values: Nietzsche's expression for the move from belief that morality is power to belief that morality is weakness. See *master morality* and *slave morality*.

Trinity (Christianity): belief that God is three-in-one: Father, Son, and Holy Ghost.

tyranny of the majority: social pressure put on individuals by the community to control their thoughts or actions.

162   GLOSSARY

"Übermensch": Nietzschean "Over-man" of pride and power, a creator of values.

"Understanding" (Emerson): External rationality and observation.

unencumbered self: conception of human beings as essentially isolated rights-possessors having no necessary relations to each other in communities.

utilitarianism: the theory that our moral obligations are always in efforts to create or produce the greatest happiness for the greatest number.

universal causation, principle of: purportedly known immediately; the claim that nothing comes from nothing, that everything must have a cause. Denies infinite regress of causes.

veil of ignorance: part of the original position in which deliberators do not know contingent facts about their own existence that will result in a fair choice procedure in deriving principles of justice.

virtue-ethics, virtue-theoretic (approaches to ethics): ethical theory concentrating on the development of human character (excellence) rather than consequences of actions.

Will to Power: Nietzsche's expression of human greatness expressed in power and the creation of values.

woman suffrage: movement to secure rights for women to vote and to participate in the political process.

REFERENCES

Adams, John. "Thoughts on Government," in *The Portable John Adams*, John Patrick Diggins (ed.). New York: Penguin Group, 2004.

———. "A Defense of the Constitutions of the United States of America," in *The Portable John Adams*, John Patrick Diggins (ed.). New York: Penguin Group, 2004.

Aristotle. *Politics*. In *The Basic Works of Aristotle*, Richard McKeon (ed.). Introduction by C. D. C. Reeve. New York: Random House, 1941.

———. *Metaphysics*. In *The Basic Works of Aristotle*, Richard McKeon (ed.). Introduction by C. D. C. Reeve. New York: Random House, 1941.

Berkeley, George. *Principles of Human Knowledge and Three Dialogues*, Roger Woolhouse (ed.). New York: Penguin, 2004.

Darwin, Charles. *On the Origin of Species by Means of Natural Selection or The Preservation of Favoured Races in the Struggle for Life*, William Bynum (ed.). New York: Penguin, 2009.

Descartes, Rene. "Meditations on First Philosophy," In *Meditations, Objections, and Replies,* Roger Ariew and Donald Cress (eds and trs.). Indianapolis, IN: Hackett Publishing Company, 2006.

Dew, Thomas. "Thomas R. Dew Defends Slavery [1852]." Available online at: www.wwnorton.com/college/history/archive/resources/documents/ch15_03.htm (accessed 9 July 2012).

Dewey, John. *Reconstruction in Philosophy*. New York: Henry Holt and Company, 1920.

———. *The Public and Its Problems*. New York: Henry Holt and Company, 1927.

Douglass, Frederick. "What to the Slave is the Fourth of July?" Available online at: http://teachingamericanhistory.org/library/index.asp?document=162 (accessed 9 July 2012).

Du Bois, W. E. B. *The Souls of Black Folk*. In *Du Bois: Writings*. New York: Penguin Books, 1986.

Edwards, Jonathan. "The Spider Letter," in *The Works of Jonathan Edwards, Vol. 6: Scientific and Philosophical Writings*, Wallace E. Anderson (ed.). New Haven: Yale University Press, 1980.

——. "A Divine and Supernatural Light," in *A Jonathan Edwards Reader*, John E. Smith, Harry S. Stout, and Kenneth P. (eds). Minkema. New Haven: Yale University Press, 1995.

——. "A Treatise Concerning Religious Affections," in *A Jonathan Edwards Reader*, John E. Smith, Harry S. Stout, and Kenneth P. Minkema (eds). New Haven: Yale University Press, 1995.

——. "Sinners in the Hands of an Angry God," in *A Jonathan Edwards Reader*, John E. Smith, Harry S. Stout, and Kenneth P. Minkema (eds). New Haven: Yale University Press, 1995.

——. *Enquiry into Freedom of the Will*. In *A Jonathan Edwards Reader*, John E. Smith, Harry S. Stout, and Kenneth P. Minkema (eds). New Haven: Yale University Press, 1995.

Emerson, Ralph Waldo, "Self-Reliance," in Ralph Waldo Emerson, *The Works of Ralph Waldo Emerson in One Volume*. Roslyn, NY: Black's Readers Service, undated.

——. "The American Scholar," in Ralph Waldo Emerson, *The Works of Ralph Waldo Emerson in One Volume*. Roslyn, NY: Black's Readers Service, undated.

——. "Divinity School Address," in Ralph Waldo Emerson, *The Portable Emerson*, Carl Bode (ed.). New York: Penguin Books, 1981.

——. "The American Scholar," in Ralph Waldo Emerson, *The Portable Emerson*, Carl Bode (ed.). New York: Penguin Books, 1981.

Franklin, Benjamin. *The Autobiography of Benjamin Franklin*. Leonard W. Labaree, Ralph L. Ketcham, Helen C. Boatfield, and Helene H. Fineman (eds). New Haven: Yale University Press, 1964.

Friedan, Betty. *The Feminine Mystique*. New York: W. W. Norton & Company, Inc., 1963.

Garrison, William Lloyd. "Declaration of Sentiments of the American Anti-Slavery Convention," in *Selections from the Writings of W. L. Garrison*. Boston: R. F. Wallcut, 1852.

Gettier, Edmund L. "Is Justified True Belief Knowledge?" *Analysis* 23 (1963): 121–3.

Gilligan, Carol. *In A Different Voice: Psychological Theory and Women's Development*. Cambridge: Harvard University Press, 1982.

Goldman, Emma. "Anarchism: What it Really Stands For," in *Anarchism and Other Essays*. Port Washington, NY: Kennikat Press, 1969. Available free online in *The Emma Goldman Papers* at http://sunsite.berkeley.edu/goldman/ (accessed 9 July 2012).

———. "Patriotism: A Menace to Liberty," in *Anarchism and Other Essays*. Port Washington, NY: Kennikat Press, 1969. Available free online in *The Emma Goldman Papers* at: http://sunsite.berkeley.edu/goldman/ (accessed 9 July 2012).

———. "Woman Suffrage," in *Anarchism and Other Essays*, Port Washington, NY: Kennikat Press, 1969. Available free online in *The Emma Goldman Papers* at: http://sunsite.berkeley.edu/goldman/ (accessed 9 July 2012).

Grimké, Angelina Emily. *Appeal to the Christian Women of the South*. Available online at: http://utc.iath.virginia.edu/abolitn/abesaegat.html (accessed 9 July 2012).

Grimké, Sarah Moore. "Letter VIII: On The Condition of Women in the United States," in Sarah Moore Grimké, *Letters on the Equality of the Sexes, and the Condition of Woman*. Boston: Isaac Knapp, 1838.

———. "Letter I: The Original Equality of Woman," in Sarah Moore Grimké, *Letters on the Equality of the Sexes, and the Condition of Woman*. Boston: Isaac Knapp, 1838.

———. "Letter IV: Social Intercourse of the Sexes," in Sarah Moore Grimké, *Letters on the Equality of the Sexes, and the Condition of Woman*. Boston: Isaac Knapp, 1838.

Harris, Leonard (ed.). *Philosophy Born of Struggle: Anthology of Afro-American Philosophy from 1917*. Dubuque, IA: Kendall/Hunt Publishing Company, 1983.

Held, Virginia. *The Ethics of Care: Personal, Political, and Global*. New York: Oxford University Press, 2006.

Hesiod. *Theogony*, in *Hesiod and Theognis*, Dorothea Wender (trs). New York: Penguin Putnam, 1973.

hooks, bell. *Feminist Theory: From Margin to Center*. Cambridge, MA: South End Press, 1984.

James, William. "The Moral Philosopher and the Moral Life." *International Journal of Ethics* 1(3) (April 1891).

———. "The Will to Believe," in *Essays in Pragmatism*. New York: Hafner Press, 1948.

———. "The Dilemma of Determinism," in *Essays in Pragmatism*. New York: Hafner Press, 1948.

———. "What Pragmatism Means," in *Essays in Pragmatism*. New York: Hafner Press, 1948.

———. "What Makes a Life Significant." Available online at: www.des.emory.edu/mfp/jsignificant.html (accessed 9 July 2012).

———. "The Moral Equivalent of War." Available online at: www.constitution.org/wj/meow.htm (accessed 9 July 2012).

Jefferson, Thomas. "The Unanimous Declaration of the Thirteen United States of America," in *Journals of Congress*. Available online at: http://memory.loc.gov/cgi-bin/ampage?collId=lljc&fileName=005/lljc005.db&recNum=94 (accessed 9 July 2012).

——. "Notes on the State of Virginia," in *The Portable Thomas Jefferson*, Merrill D. Peterson (ed.). New York: Penguin Books, 1975.

——. "A Bill for Establishing Religious Freedom," in *The Portable Thomas Jefferson*, Merrill D. Peterson (ed.). New York: Penguin Books, 1975.

——. *The Jefferson Bible: The Life and Morals of Jesus of Nazareth*. Radford, VA: Wilder Publications, 2007.

Kant, Immanuel. "Answer to the Question: What is Enlightenment?", Thomas K. Abbot (tr). Intr. by Allen W. Wood, in *Basic Writings of Kant*. New York: Modern Library, 2001.

King, Martin Luther, Jr. *Letter from the Birmingham Jail*. Available online at: www.mlkonline.net/jail.html (accessed 9 July 2012).

Kuhn, Thomas. *The Structure of Scientific Revolutions*. Chicago: University of Chicago Press, 1962.

Locke, John. *An Essay Concerning Human Understanding*, Vols. I and II. Alexander Campbell Fraser (ed.). New York: Dover Publications, 1959.

Madison, James. "Federalist 10" and "Federalist 51." in *The Federalist Papers Reader and Historical Documents of Our American Heritage*, Frederick Quinn (ed.). Santa Ana, CA: Seven Locks Press, 1997.

Mill, John Stuart. *On Liberty*. Elizabeth Rapaport (ed.). Indianapolis: Hackett, 1978.

Nietzsche, Friederich. *On the Genealogy of Morals*. In *Basic Writings of Nietzsche*, Walter Kaufmann (ed. and trs.). New York: Modern Library, 1968.

——. "Thus Spoke Zarathustra," in *The Portable Nietzsche*, Walter Kaufmann (tr. and ed.). New York: Penguin Group, 1976.

Nozick, Robert. *Anarchy, State, and Utopia*. New York: Basic Books, 1974.

Paine, Thomas. *African Slavery in America*. Available online at: www.constitution.org/tp/afri.htm (accessed 9 July 2012).

——. "Common Sense," in Thomas Paine, *Common Sense and Other Political Writings*, Nelson F. Adkins (ed.). Indianapolis: The Bobbs–Merrill Company, 1953.

——. "The American Crisis," in Thomas Paine, *Common Sense and Other Political Writings*, Nelson F. Adkins (ed.). Indianapolis: The Bobbs–Merrill Company, 1953.

——. "The Rights of Man," in Thomas Paine, *Common Sense and Other Political Writings*, Nelson F. Adkins (ed.). Indianapolis: The Bobbs–Merrill Company, 1953.

——. *The Age of Reason, Part I*. Second Edn. Aulburey Castell (ed.). Indianapolis: Library of Liberal Arts, 1957.

Peirce, Charles Sanders. "What Pragmatism Is," *The Monist* 15(2) (April 1905): 161–81 and available online at: www.cspeirce.com/menu/library/bycsp/ whatis/whatpragis.htm (accessed 9 July 2012).

——. "The Fixation of Belief," in Charles Sanders Peirce, *Philosophical Writings of Peirce*, Justus Buchler (ed.). New York: Dover Publications, 1955.

——. "How to Make Our Ideas Clear," in Charles Sanders Peirce, *Philosophical Writings of Peirce*, Justus Buchler (ed.). New York: Dover Publications, 1955.

Quine, Willard Van Orman. "Two Dogmas of Empiricism," in *From a Logical Point of View*. Cambridge, MA: Harvard University Press, 1953.

Rawls, John. "Justice as Fairness," *The Philosophical Review*, 7(2) (April 1958): 164–94.

——. *A Theory of Justice*. Cambridge, MA: Harvard University Press, 1971.

Rorty, Richard. *Philosophy and the Mirror of Nature*. Princeton, NJ: Princeton University Press, 1979.

——. *Philosophy and Social Hope*. New York: Penguin Books, 1999.

Sandel, Michael J. "The Procedural Republic and the Unencumbered Self," *Political Theory* 12(1) (February 1984): 81–96.

——. *Democracy's Discontent: American in Search of a Public Philosophy*. Cambridge, MA: Harvard University Press, 1996.

——. *Public Philosophy*. Cambridge, MA: Harvard University Press, 2006.

Santayana, George. "Public Opinion," in *The Essential Santayana: Selected Writings*. Bloomington, IN: Indiana UP, 2009.

Stanlick, Nancy A. and Bruce S. Silver. *Philosophy in America: Volumes I and II*. Upper Saddle River, NJ: Pearson Prentice Hall, 2004.

Stanton, Elizabeth Cady. "The Matriarchate or Mother-Age: An Address of Mrs. Stanton Before the National Council of Women," February 1891. *National Bulletin*, 1891.

——. "The Solitude of Self," in *Elizabeth Cady Stanton and Susan B. Anthony: Correspondence, Writings, and Speeches*, Ellen Carol DuBois (ed.). New York: Schocken Books, 1987.

——. *The Woman's Bible*. Amherst, NY: Prometheus Books, 1999.

Thoreau, Henry David. "Resistance to Civil Government," *The Writings of Henry D. Thoreau: Reform Papers*, Wendell Glick (ed.). Princeton: Princeton University Press, 1973.

——. *Walden*, Jeffrey S. Cramer (ed.). New York: Penguin Books, 2012.

West, Cornel. *Prophesy Deliverance! An Afro-American Revolutionary Christianity*. Louisville, KY: Westminster John Knox Press, 1982.

——. *Race Matters*. Boston, MA: Beacon Press, 1993.

Wright, Chauncey. *The Philosophical Writings of Chauncey Wright*, Edward H. Madden (ed.). New York: The American Heritage Series, 1958.

INDEX

Free Will in *The Basics*

Free Will: The Basics

Meghan Griffith, Davidson College, USA

"This is an absolutely wonderful introductory book on the issues surrounding the very lively debates about free will and moral responsibility. The author has a gift for getting right to the heart of the issues. I highly recommend this book."

John Martin Fischer, *University of California Riverside, USA*

The question of whether humans are free to make their own decisions has long been contested and it continues to be a controversial topic today. *Free Will: The Basics* provides readers with a clear and accessible introduction to this central philosophical debate. It examines key questions such as:

- Does free will exist or is it an illusion?
- Is it possible to have free will if everything is determined?
- Can moral responsibility exist without free will?
- What can recent scientific developments tell us about the existence of free will?

With detailed examples, a glossary of terms and suggestions for further study, *Free Will: The Basics* addresses the key debates without prejudice and is an essential read for anyone wishing to explore this challenging philosophical problem.

December 2012 – 150 pages
Pb: 978-0-415-56220-1- Hb: 978-0-415-56219-5

For more information and to order a copy visit:
http://www.routledge.com/9780415562201

Available from all good bookshops